# Encinitas

## Our History and People

By

Carolyn Roy Cope, Jim Filanc and Garth Murphy

Published by Ledge Media & HPN Books, a division of FRE-Enterprises, Jackson, Wyoming

# Legacy Sponsors

Through their generous support, the following companies helped make this project possible.

**The Ecke Family**
7220 Avenida Encinas, Suite 204
Carlsbad, CA 92011

Charlie's Foreign Car

**Charlie's Foreign Car**
751 2nd Street
Encinitas, CA 92024
(760) 753-4969
www.charliesforeigncar.com

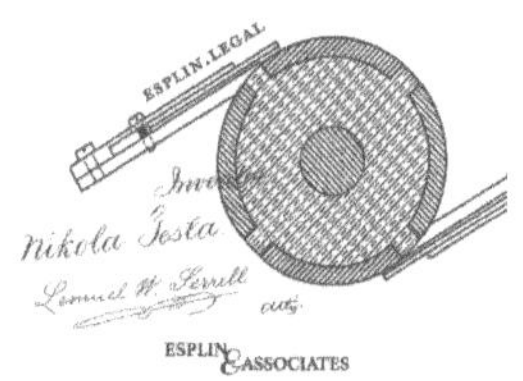


**Esplin & Associates**
206 4th Street
Encinitas, CA 92024
(760) 249-2133
www.esplin.legal

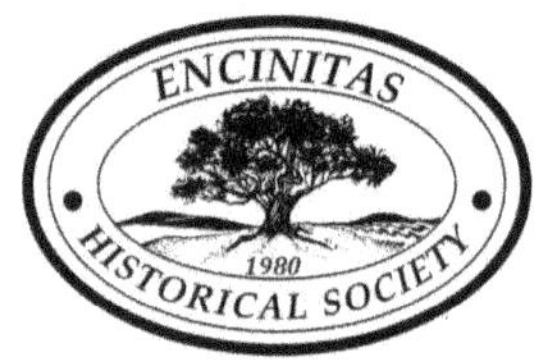


**Encinitas Historical Society**
390 West F Street
Encinitas, CA 92024
(760) 942-9066
www.encinitashistoricalsociety.org

---

Second Edition Abridged


ISBN: 979-8-89177-003-4
LCCN: 2023945095

**Encinitas: Our History and People**

*authors:* Carolyn Roy Cope, Jim Filanc and Garth Murphy
*cover artist:* Kevin Anderson
*project manager and managing editor:* Daphne Fletcher
*contributing writers for "Sharing the Heritage":* Kevin Kern, Kyle Thomas and Sid Shapira
*contributing photographers:* Daphne Fletcher, Kyle Thomas and Neal Glasgow

**HPNbooks**

*publisher & CEO:* Daphne Fletcher
*director of IT:* Rafael Ramirez
*administration:* Donna Mata, Kristin T. Williamson
*production:* Colin Hart, Christopher D. Sturdevant

# Dedication

*"Socially distanced" 2020 gathering of the Encinitas Historical Society Board of Directors.*

PHOTO COURTESY OF DAPHNE FLETCHER.

HISTORICAL SOCIETY BOARD OF DIRECTORS

Carolyn Cope
Lois Aufmann
Dayna Donatelli
Jim Filanc
Marilyn Fowler
Liz Kovack
Joy Lyndes
Gigi Lopatriello
Connie McIntire
Suzanne Spector
Adrien Spector
Mike and Terri Wallace
Pam Hammond Walker

SOURCES

"Profiles in Flowers," by Robert Melvin
"Encinitas History & Heritage," by Mac Hartley
"San Dieguito Heritage," by Maura Wiegand, Ph.D
"Encinitas Magazine," publisher Jim Baumann
"Santa Fe Coast Lines Depot," by Serpico and Gustafson
"Goat Roping and a Town Called Merle," Kathie Jenuine
"Images of America: Encinitas," by Kenneth Holtzclaw and Diane Welch
"Images of America: Cardiff-by-the-Sea," by Wehtahnah Tucker and Gus Bujkovsky
"Brief History of Encinitas," by Annie Hammond Cozens
"Colony Olivenhain," by Richard Bumann
Encinitas Historical Society Archives

# Contents

# Acknowledgements


Garth Murphy
Lloyd O'Connell
Mrs. Jan Grice
Pamela Hammond Walker
Irene Kratzer
Teresa Arballo Barth
Susan Hays
Richard and "Twink" Bumann
Charles Marvin III

Dave Oakley
Rachel Brupbacher:
(Great-Grand Niece to Miles Justus Kellogg)
Lorraine Anne Eden:
(Grand-Daughter of J. Frank Cullen)
Fred Caldwell
Jim Filanc
Sonja Holtman
Lois and Richard Aufmann


This timeline and publication is as historically accurate as possible using the sources mentioned on the previous page, along with personal interviews, and on-line documents to verify and validate facts, locations and events. The publisher and the Encinitas Historical Society are not liable for any errors or omissions.

PHOTO BY TO BETSY O'NEIL.

# INTRODUCTION

BY CATHERINE SMITH BLAKESPEAR
MAYOR, CITY OF ENCINITAS

When my family first moved to the area that would become Encinitas nearly 100 years ago in the 1920s, they undoubtedly were drawn to the same magical qualities that capture our individual and collective imaginations today. Those intangibles define the place that is Encinitas—the soft, slight coolness on the breeze, even on the hottest day; the variety in our eclectic built environment created incrementally over many decades; the glow reflected from the seaside bluffs at sunset onto our sandy beaches; the lagoons that meet the oceans bookending the undulating sandstone ecology; the touch and smell of our plants, reflecting both the desert and the tropics; and most importantly the historic, founding roots of the community created by our original families. These provide the mooring for our present-day city and its culture.

My great-grandma's family moved to Encinitas, an area that was then known as San Dieguito, from the greater Los Angeles area in order to plant, harvest, and sell flowers. Born in 1917, my grandma Dorothea Patricia Smith described many times how flower growing was the ideal business to weather the Great Depression. Even in down times, "people will still get married and die," she'd say, ensuring a steady source of flower-buying customers.

Encinitas has several well-known historic flower-growing families, most prominent the Paul Ecke family, who hybridized and mass marketed the Poinsettia flower during the 1950s. Thanks to the impact of newly colorized televisions and immensely popular shows, including the Bob Hope Christmas specials, the bright red Encinitas-grown poinsettia became the flower indelibly linked to the holidays throughout the United States and the world.

*The 2021 Encinitas City Council raising the flag, from left to right: Joy Lyndes, Tony Kranz, Mayor Catherine S. Blakespear, Joe Mosca, and Kellie Hinze*

In addition to the pioneering Ecke family, there were dozens of smaller flower-growing players, like my grandma's family. She and her family would get up in the stillness of the pre-dawn hours to drive their flowers—mainly gladiolas, which she called "glads"—to the Los Angeles Flower Market. Long after many types of flowers had moved indoors to be nurtured safely within greenhouses, gladiolas remained a local outdoor row crop.

Over the last 70 years—from the post-war 1950s boom to the go-go 1980s and through to the slower-growth movements of today—Encinitas has experienced nothing short of a complete transformation. Instead of growing plants, the land now sprouts homes and businesses. But the essence of our beloved hometown remains resolutely intact.

As Encinitas transformed, my family mirrored its path over four generations. While my great-grandparents were flower farmers, my grandparents moved into construction. Their family business, "Smith Construction Company" was the largest employer in Cardiff in the 1950s, building schools, bowling alleys, and roads. My parents pursued professional degrees to become attorneys; and I work as the mayor of the City of Encinitas and also as a practicing attorney. The question for all of us is the same—what will my children, and our city's children, do and become? What will Encinitas do and become?

I believe that the key to the healthy, long-term evolution of the City of Encinitas is our community's reckoning with its inevitable growth. Together, we are committed to preserving the magical essence that defines Encinitas. Our challenge is to shape the future to ensure our vitality and continued high standard of living. At nearly every stage, the sentimental reflection on an idyllic past can thwart the best-intentioned efforts toward beneficial change. The art of positive progress lies in the delicate balancing of both preservation and enhancement.

With our future in mind, the city in 2019 has dedicated itself to providing more homes for residents at all income levels, with a particular focus on housing for middle and low-income workers. A vibrant city accounts for all its residents; it does not shut the door on people.

We are also conscientiously working to maximize the potential of our historic rail corridor for transportation, the economy, recreation and pleasure. The railroad laid down its first tracks in the 1880s, literally putting Encinitas on the map between the Mexican border and Los Angeles. Now, almost 150 years later, living with a railroad that bifurcates our coastal community increasingly challenges Encinitas to get creative when it comes to sharing physical and auditory space, and facilitating the flow of residents across and through this busy corridor, whether on bike, foot, train or in a car.

In order to improve our city's environment, and the health of our largest eco-system, the planet, Encinitas has committed to an ambitious program of greatly reducing the amount of emissions we produce. Our lauded "gold-standard" climate action plan relies on more bike lanes and walking paths, more trees, less driving, more recycled water and cleaner power sources.

When the people of Encinitas came together in 1986 and decided at the ballot box to become an incorporated city instead of an insignificant part of San Diego County, we laid claim to our right to self-determination. Now in our five distinct communities—Old Encinitas, Leucadia, Cardiff-by-the-Sea, New Encinitas, and Olivenhain—we continue to define for ourselves our shared future and how our city looks and feels.

This photo journal reminds us of the historic and diverse cloth that created the present; it's a colorful tapestry that we're all a part of today. Looking back is a soul-nourishing pleasure, and importantly it provides the insight we need when we face forward. As we walk the path to the future together, I have no doubt that Encinitas will continue its dynamic evolution, inspired by the footsteps of those who came before us.

*Catherine Blakespear's family: uncle, Raymond Elstad; aunt, Rosemary Kimbal; grandmother, Dorothea P. Smith (seated in the chair); mother, Tricia A. Smith; step-father Richard Cottrell; Catherine Blakespear; son, Oliver; daughter, Ava; and husband, Jeremy.*

PHOTO COURTESY OF RAYMOND ELSTAD.

✧

*An artistic "then and now" look at Encinitas, the murals can be found at on the 7-11 building at D Street and 101 by Artist Micaiah Hardison.*

IMAGE COURTESY OF DAPHNE FLETCHER.

# CHAPTER 1

## IN THE BEGINNING: THE EARLY YEARS

BY GARTH MURPHY, NATIVE AMERICAN HISTORIAN

The people we call Native Americans arrived in Southern California at least 13,000 years ago. They came on foot from the north, crossing from Siberia on a snow-covered land bridge during the last ice age, when the sea levels were 30 to 100 feet lower than today. "The People", as Native Americans called themselves, rapidly spread east and south, from Nova Scotia to Tierra Del Fuego at the tip of South America—still walking—horses would come later with the Spanish. San Diego County became a permanent home for these nomadic people. This area offered a temperate climate; seven major rivers flowed from the Sierra to the sea with a natural wealth of available animal and plant food on the land from the rivers. Estuaries and the ocean provided enough to support a healthy population of tribal bands speaking five distinct dialects and numbering in the tens of thousands.

*By the late 1700s, the Native American population of the Encinitas region numbered tens of thousands. The native town of Hakutl near Moonlight Beach at the mouth of Cottonwood Creek, between the Kumayaay and Luiseno tribes. The Hakuti were close enough to Batiquitos and San Elijo Lagoons to harvest their estuaries' bounty of fish, shellfish and fowl.*

ARTIST MICAIAH HARDISON

In the north county there were 111 native townships when the Spanish arrived in 1769, according to Spanish Mission records from San Luis Rey. This territory included Encinitas. A native village called Hakutl centered on Moonlight Beach at the mouth of Cottonwood Creek. There were other large villages nearby. The Jeyal people settled at the back of San Elijo Lagoon and the Ajopunguile at the east end of Batiquitos Lagoon. Fresh water flowed into the brackish estuaries that define Encinitas' current boundaries.

The Hakutl people found the area special because they had a permanent spring-fed creek that provided sweet fresh water directly into the sea—no lagoon. The Hakutl people could thrive at the

Artist's renderings of Native Americans who inhabited the Encinitas area.

ILLUSTRATIONS BY DAVID HOUSE.

ocean's edge. Hakutl people were still close enough to Batiquitos and San Elijo lagoons to harvest the estuaries' bounty of fish, shellfish and fowl without having to deal with the torrential winter floodwaters that came from these larger rivers. Hakutl also had west facing and frost free highlands where Cottonwood Creek traverses its way to the beach. A temperate year-round micro-climate extended from lagoon to lagoon. All of this made for a pleasant living environment in recyclable grass huts.

The natives of Hakutl lived very close to the ill-defined border between the two great coastal tribes, the Kumayaay, or Diegano, what the Spanish called them. The Luiseño, the northern tribe, were associated with the San Luis Rey Mission whose territories extended east to the Sierra and north to Rancho Santa Margarita y Las Flores, now Camp Pendleton. The Kumayaay occupied a vast tract straddling the border from Ensenada to the San Dieguito River, just three miles south of Encinitas. The eastern tribes were the Yuman, Kuupiaxchem, and the Cahuilla whose territories covered the east side of Sierra to the Colorado River.

By 1769 these tribes were no longer nomadic. The land was rich and they did not have to go far for food. The tribes lived at peace most of the time as tribal skirmishes were sporadic and short lived. The People moved within their boundaries seasonally, mountains to the sea trading food, tools, shells, beads and seeds. Native villages and tribal bands were run as simple democracies with elected chiefs for both men and woman. A large tribe was divided into moieties. There were two groups, the

coyotes and the wild cats, best described as fraternal orders. Marriage had to be with a member of the opposite group.

Hakutl residents, as with other San Diego natives, cultivated and consumed the acorn. This nutty seed of the oak tree provided their diets with a calorie-rich staple. Acorns were soaked to remove the bitter tannins, dried and ground on a stone to create a flour to make nutritious porridge or patties roasted on a fire heated rock. The acorn diet staple was augmented with creek-side greens, berries, roots and grass seeds, as well as game birds. They hunted animals large and small from rats, possums and rabbits to antelope, deer and elk. The valley east of the Hakutl village held the big game and the huge oaks produced bushels of acorns. The wild back country valleys were also grizzly bear and mountain lion habitats. The bears were respected by The People as equals and were not hunted. California's state flag carries the extinct grizzly bear's image in their honor, a surviving vestige of this native cultural ethos.

Horticulture practiced by The People of Hakutl included controlled burning to preserve the oaks and to aid in grass seed collection for trading and planting. A symbolic handful of seeds were given to a bride when asked to marry. Woman did most of the planting, harvesting and gathering. Hakutl women would gather supplies in a flexible bag each day with the natural resources that provided about 65% of their diet. Women did the food preparation as well as house building and maintenance and production of their clothing. In a society where all movement was on foot, mobility and safety depended on everyone being able to walk and carry something. Bands of The People would gather at the coast just south of Hakutl for the yearly Torrey Pines

*Reproductions of early Native American dwellings can be found at the San Diego Botanic Gardens and at the San Dieguito Heritage Museum.*

✧

*This "wikiup" is an example of a typical coastal Indian dwelling found around Encinitas.*

Festival when the pine cones were ripe. There they could socialize, find mates, trade and feast on the fatty Torrey Pine nuts that grew nowhere else on California's mainland. Such events were also a chance to discuss the alarming invasion of white and black immigrants. They developed a code of smoke signals to identify the arrival of ships. The Hakutl had prime sea observation posts from the tall seaside bluffs.

The Spanish and their missionaries ruled California and the Hakutl from 1769 to 1822. During those 53 years the missionaries and the missions were controlled by Spanish king's agents. The goal of the Padres was to convert the natives to Christianity, educate them and make them servants of the king. Under Mission rule, the isolated native population in San Diego County had been severely depleted by invasive European diseases. Population fell from 20,000 to 5,000 in 1822. During a 24 year period from 1822 to 1846, known as the Mexican Rancho Period, the Californios ruled themselves. The Missions of San Diego and San Luis Rey created twenty-two land grant ranches. Rancho Encinitas was one of those land grants owned by the Ybarra Family. The People of Hakutl, now part of Rancho Encinitas, worked at the haciendas as ranch hands or servants. This was a low point for a proud race. In 1846 the Americans conquered California with an army of 120 men and a few naval warships. In 1848 the signing of the treaty of Guadalupe-Hidalgo gave all Mexicans in California US citizenship. Many educated natives claimed their rights too. That same year the discovery of gold began the rapacious California Gold Rush. The first census in 1850, after California became a state, there were reported only 30,000 natives left in the entire state...down from 400 thousand.

Oak trees in Spanish are encinos. Encinitas means little live oaks after those important oak trees that flourished in abundance along Cottonwood Creek and the surrounding valleys. Encinitas became a platted township thirty-three years later in 1883. Permanent fresh water, along with plenty of oak firewood, the first steam engine train arrived in Encinitas.

The Hakutl people were gone for good.

*Top:.Because of our coastal desert climate, the natives did not need to wear layers of clothing. Very little coverings were required for both men and women.*

COURTESY OF GARTH MURPHY.

*Bottom: A gathering place for women preparing acorn, nuts and herbs using the metate (mealing stone).*

COURTESY OF THE SAN DIEGUITO HERITAGE MUSEUM AT HERITAGE RANCH

*Top and bottom: Early Native American mortar and pestle exhibit.*

COURTESY OF THE SAN DIEGUITO HERITAGE MUSEUM AT HERITAGE RANCH

# CHAPTER 2

## ENCINITAS IS BORN: 1850-1899

By the time California became the 31st state of the Union in 1850, Encinitas as we now know it started to take shape. America continued to move west, bringing innovation and new settlers looking for a new place to call home. Early outposts in what were to become Leucadia, Encinitas, Olivenhain and Cardiff started to appear. By the time the 1880s rolled around, the region started to see accelerated growth, led by the new Santa Fe railroad. Encinitas' first school house, our beloved 1883 school house, was built. The early settlements of Olivenhain and Leucadia started to take root. Agriculture started to develop, boosting the local economy.

*The 1800 Schoolhouse. The original one room schoolhouse sat neatly atop the highest part of the western bluff. Originally the building faced east to west with the doors facing east. Two doors, one for girls and one for boys. When the building was moved back to its current location it had to face south to north, although only 100 feet from its original location.*

✧

*Above: Peter Lux.*

*Below: Early Encinitas.*

1850 ➤
- California becomes the 31st state on September 9th.

1869 ➤
- Encinitas stagecoach station is established along *El Camino Real* (King's Highway).

1870 ➤
- Leucadia Roadside Park is created. This is the oldest park in Leucadia. It was once known as "Spirit Woods". It is reputed to have been the outdoor meeting place for the English Spiritualists, a very popular movement in the mid-1800s.

1875 ➤
- Nathan Eaton, a New Yorker, is the first to settle on the south shore of Batiquitos Slough in Leucadia. He is a successful bee keeper and names his plot of land Eatonsville but is often referred to by locals as Eaton's Canyon.
- Hector and Sara Cray MacKinnon (and three toddlers) homestead 600 acres two miles south of Encinitas near San Elijo Lagoon from the beach to what is now I-5 in Cardiff. They are instrumental in developing a school there. The first classes are held in their barn. Hector sells some of his land to James Frank Cullen, a painter from Boston, who also becomes a developer.

1880s ➤
- Lemuel Cornell Kincaid, a conductor for Santa Fe Railroad, is the second settler in the Leucadia area. He homesteads the property where the Paul Ecke ranch is eventually established along Saxony Road.

1881 ➤
- Encinitas is born! (named after the coastal scrub oak *encinitos*) California Southern Railroad directs Thomas Rattan to lay out the town of Encinitas.
- John Pitcher and Thomas Rattan are recognized as "Encinitas Founders".

1882 ➤

- A school district is established. The founders pass a $600 bond at 6% to build the schoolhouse for grades 1-8. Twelve votes were needed and passed unanimously.
- Merle is another name used for Leucadia. E.B. Scott's second son's name is Merle. E.B. Scott also builds the Merle post office (that may have been at Vulcan and Hillcrest area). A little shack in a clearing was the first school. There were only fifteen students. Last known use of the name Merle is in 1947. It opened on July 1, 1894, and closed in 1910.
- The Railroad comes through Encinitas for the first time on August 14th. The population at that time was only eleven.

*Top, left: The Green Valley route for El Camino Real.*

*Top, right: A summer harvest.*

*Below: Hammond Family Ranch.*

1883 ➤

- John Pitcher buys half of Encinitas and gifts 2.25 acres for a new schoolhouse.
- Edward Graham Hammond and Jane Latchford Hammond family arrive on May 8th with their seven children, Thomas Latchford (Jane's father) and Harry Carter. The arrival doubles the population from 11 to 22. The only buildings in town are the combination grocery store/ticket office and three section houses where Ben Elliott and the Chinese rail workers live. These were built by Ruben and Sue Chaffin not only manages the store but also sells train tickets and is the post-mistress. Most of the Hammonds settle in the area that eventually becomes part of the Paul Ecke Ranch. There they establish the Hammond Sunset Ranch complete with a natural spring fed artesian pond, which is still there today. (southeast corner of Quail Gardens Dr. & Leucadia Blvd). Edward Hammond is also an experienced cabinet maker. He constructs several buildings in the community, including the first dedicated school building, the Pitcher House Hotel and the Derby House (649 South Vulcan Avenue.)
- One-Room Schoolhouse (390 W. F St) is built by Mr. Edward G. Hammond and his 17-year-old son Edward "Ted". John Pitcher had already personally gifted this land at 3rd and "E" Streets specifically for a school on March 8th. This 900 square foot building is made mostly out of redwood with fir for the flooring, using handmade square nails. The "desks" are slab tables with redwood benches. In 1890 "combined desks" replace the slab benches. Seventeen children attend the first class. It is currently the oldest building still standing in Encinitas, maintained by the Encinitas Historical Society.
- James Benjamin Elliott, a railroad foreman, directs Chinese train laborers in planting acres of Eucalyptus trees shipped from Australia. Eucalyptus and Cypress trees are planted in Leucadia from 1885-1900.

*Originally known as Noonan's Point this impressive piece of land became the property of the Self Realization Fellowship in 1936 when it was purchased as a gift for Paramahansa Yogananda for his private hermitage.*

1884 ➤ • Great Flood-No Trains! In February, heavy winter rains wash out 30 miles of the train tracks in the Temecula Valley. For nine months there is no rail communication to Encinitas. The Chaffin's grocery store begins to run out of food.
- Everyone shares what they have and made their supplies last.
- German Colony Olivenhain is officially formed on May 21st. Sixty-seven new German colonists arrive on November 8th. Lack of water is not what they expected. Over the next few years Colony Olivenhain population peaks at 310. By 1887 only 80 people remain.

1885 ➤ • Leucadia is named after the Greek Isle Lefkada in the Ionian island chain. The name means "bright & shining isle of paradise" or "sheltered paradise" or "place of refuge". These all have been noted to be the translation to describe this area by the English Spiritualists who settled here. Surveyor, Mr. D.N. Sanford, names the streets and a pantheon of Greek gods and Roman deity names are scattered throughout Leucadia. By 1898 there is a schoolhouse, a church and a railroad stop in the Vulcan and Hillcrest area.
- The Germania Hotel is constructed for $500 as a private residence in Olivenhain by Herman Baecht and his family of twelve. It is eventually moved to the Olivenhain Meeting Hall property in 1982. Restoration the home/hotel is complete.

*Looking west towards the ocean, this is the first "downtown" picture showing the one room schoolhouse, the church and the almost completed train station.*

1886 ➤ • Olivenhain School opens in Theodore Pinther's old house and is used until 1888.
- Herman Bumann homesteads 160 acres in Olivenhain. The buildings are preserved to this day by his descendants.

✧

*Top: The Derby House.*

*Bottom: The Hammond Sunset Ranch, c. 1890. Rows of apple trees along what would become El Camino Real in what was then known as Green Valley.*

1887 ➤

- Derby House (649 S. Vulcan) is built by Edward Hammond for railroad man Amos Gates Derby, his wife and four daughters. The completed 5,600 sq. foot house made of redwood has seven bedrooms, a central dining room and a red brick fireplace. The combined dining and living room ran the length of the home. The built-in cabinets were beautifully handcrafted. It has not only been a house but also a hotel for railroad travelers. During WWII it was "some sort of hospital". At one time "THE HOME" was painted on the slanted roof and was dedicated to the Eternal Brotherhood. It was a 14-room boarding house when purchased in 1976 and is still privately owned.
- Encinitas Community Church (560 3rd St) is built on donated land by John Pritcher and financed by the community. Later, it was moved to San Marcos.

1887-88 ➤ • The Encinitas Train Station (directly west of the Derby House) is built, along with many other downtown stores. This period is referred to as "The Boom Years." Over time the number of rail cars needed is greatly reduced and the station is permanently closed January 24, 1969.

• Noonan's Point is purchased by James Noonan for $1,000 for the ten acres. He hires Edward Hammond and his son, Ted, to build their cliff-side home. The Noonan's raise seven children there. On a September night in 1893 the house burns to the ground and the Noonan's move away. (This 10-acre ocean bluff property, known as Noonan's Point, is purchased in 1936 and the hermitage for Paramahansa Yogananda is built.)

1888 ➤ • Olivenhain One-Room School is purchased from Fred Balzer. It is moved to the southwest corner of 7th and Cole Ranch Road and remains active for fifty-four years. It was then moved to the San Dieguito High School campus and used as a class room before being demolished in the mid 1960s.

1890 ➤ • Cozens House (112 "C" Street) is built by Tom and Annie Cozens. Edward G. Hammond helped his son-in-law and daughter build their home originally near the bluff at "F" Street. In 1900, over a two-week period, they literally move the house to where it is now just above Cottonwood Creek. There Tom could dig a well in the small canyon below where the fresh water could be pumped .

• South Bay Shooting Club is built on Hillcrest Street in Leucadia by Fred Coutts.

*Left: The Cozens original house location on the bluff located approximately at 4th and "G" Streets prior to its move to just above and south of Cottonwood Creek where it sits today.*

*Bottom: The Cozens house today.*

✧

*Eucalyptus trees such as these were the source of many ties used in the local railroads. Eucalyptus trees lined the highways. These beautiful tree canopies provided shade and offered up the most pleasing aroma. Unfortunately, most succumbed to bark beetle, high winds, and street improvements.*

1893 ➤

- Fred and Anna Teten, purchase from the colony Theodore Pinther's vacated 1885 house. For a while, Pinther's house was used as the San Dieguito Valley One-Room Schoolhouse. In 1895 another vacated house is combined to it adding to the square footage. This structure was saved by the San Dieguito Heritage Museum and is now wonderfully restored on the museum property on Quail Gardens Drive and is known as "The Teten House."

1894 ➤

- Olivenhain Town Hall (423 Rancho Santa Fe Road) is constructed to celebrate the colonist's ten-year anniversary. In 1916 a kitchen and bathroom are added from the wood from the dismantled Owl Club building increasing the size to 28 feet by 36 feet. A new floor and much needed upgrades happen in 1928. Business meetings and social gatherings including picnics, celebrations, dances and weddings are among the many events that still take place there. This historic building is maintained by the Olivenhain Town Council.

1895 ➤

- Green Valley One-Room School is located north of Olivenhain Road. The building is removed when El Camino Real is widened in 1966.

1987-1917 ➤

- The Copper Creek Mine was active with two shafts, 140 feet and 400 feet.

## OLIVENHAIN

Olivenhain, "olive grove", is a beautiful name with a contrary meaning. Open spaces and lots of it...land as far as the eye could see. A man could homestead 160 acres. Many tough families did try to make a go of it growing the "promised" olives, but alas there was a lack sufficient water. This land was more arid than grove-like. Five years later the population dropped from three hundred-ten new settlers down to just eighty die-hard farmers who chose to remain on the parched land. Wells were dug, but eventually dry farming was introduced with lima beans. Springing up over the rolling hills came shanties, a local school, a town hall and a hotel. Some of the descendants of those hearty early Olivenhain pioneers still live in the area. They hold the rights to be buried in their own private cemetery. The Olivenhain Town Hall is still the center piece of community activity. Locals gather yearly to celebrate their German roots with an authentic Oktoberfest. Water did eventually come via the pipe-line, but not until 1961. Immediately the area boomed. Large estates replaced grasslands and fields. The Colony Olivenhain still has a farm feeling though with horses, goats, turkeys, chickens and a few cattle in the back yards of many of the properties on this quiet rolling "back county".

*The Olivenhain Town Hall, built in 1894, was the main gathering place for settlers. It was placed on the National Register of Historic Places in 1993.*

✧

*Above: Dressed in their Sunday best, these early pioneers pose in typical attire.*

*Right: Farmers bringing cattle to the once free flowing La Bajada Creek.*

Top: Miles Justus Kellogg's home on Second Street. Note the Boat Houses in the upper right-hand corner.

Above: A formal portrait of Miles Justus Kellogg.

Left: Local miners finishing a shift at The Copper Creek Mine, operating from 1897 to 1917.

*Early image of Encinitas farmers.*

## RANCHO DE LOS ENCINITOS

Rancho de los Encinitos, a Mexican land-grant of one square league or 4,431-03 acres, was given to Andrés Ybarra by Governor Alvarado on July 3, 1842, and a United States land-patent was granted on April 18, 1871. Being halfway between the mission at San Diego and that of San Luis Rey, it proved to be a convenient stage station, where horses were changed. In later years, it became a train stop for the California Southern Railroad.

Attention was drawn to the ranch when an ostrich farm was established there. On February 21, 1884, the National City Record said: "The ostriches have laid 10 eggs since they arrived at Encinitas. The boss egg weighed 3 lbs. and 11 oz." The ostrich venture must have been of short duration, for on August 24 of the same year, Kimball Brothers ran an advertisement in the San Diego Union: "Rancho Encinitas, 4,400 acres. The best ranch for its size for a Colony." Colonization was a favorite method for settling land, during that period.

The advertisement was answered by Theodore Pinther, favorably known in Colorado, who was planning to organize a colony. With several others, Pinther arrived in San Diego September 27, and Frank Kimball showed them several locations. "Took the party to Jamul," he noted in his records, "Also to Otay and then went to Encinitas and examined the springs in the northeast corner; then went down the east side to the southeast corner, then up to the location of the dam across Elijo Creek, through the valley and nearly to the ocean. The stage overtook us at San Dieguito, and we came home." Two days later he recorded: "At work on the Pinther Colony scheme." The following day the National City Record mentions the name of the colony at Encinitas as "Olivenhain."

On October 3 Kimball was in San Diego and saw the Articles of Incorporation for the Colony and received $400 to bind the bargain on the sale of the Encinitas Rancho for $65,000. The contract was made by Pinther, Conrad Stroebel, Paul Flossig and others. So began the Olivenhain venture; shortly afterward, a courageous little group left their homes in Colorado, for the new colony. On November 8 Kimball noted that he had "Carried apples to the first installment of Colony Olivenhain which came down by steamer. Consisted of some 60 persons, including children."

# CHAPTER 3

## ENCINITAS GROWS UP: 1900-1919

El Camino Real (The Kings Highway) has grown to become the central route for travel and commerce. The railroad continues to grow, connecting the region with the rest of the state. The economy continues to expand with the harvesting of kelp as another cash crop supporting the area. Cardiff is starting to become the community we know today. Electricity comes to the region, providing light and energy to fuel the next wave of development for the region.

*Above: A typical foggy morning along the south bound train tracks rolling into Encinitas.*

1905 ➤

- El Camino Real is now the main road going north to south.
- Lima Beans are introduced as a dry farm crop in Olivenhain. The fields would get enough moisture from the coastal mist for the lima bean crops to survive. Lima bean farming became extremely successful and annually farmed for over 50 years.

1906 ➤

- Southern California Railroad becomes a subsidiary of The Acheson, Topeka & Santa Fe Railroads.

*Right: Early settlers built small wooden homes dotting the landscape from the coast to Olivenhain.*

*Bottom: Early Cardiff looking north. Note the historic Cardiff Mercantile Building to the right.*

1908 ➤ • Lone Jack Road has a very interesting history. A real estate salesman named Mr. Muir purchased a 160-acre homestead in Olivenhain. His ranch has a few head of cattle and a mule named Jack. One hot, dry and windy day, a wildfire starts to sweep across the ranch. Muir tries to get Jack across a narrow canyon to head off the cattle. Jack won't move. Suddenly the canyon flashes into flames! He realizes then that Jack has saved his life. Out of respect, Muir names his ranch then the road after Jack. Muir sells the ranch in 1915, but the name sticks.

1909 ➤ • Encinitas Schoolhouse Annex is added to the 1883 one room school. This new entry addition is used for coats, books and teacher materials.

*Above: The trains started coming through Encinitas for the first time on August 14, 1882. The Hammond Family arrived with eleven members on May 8, 1883, literally doubling the population.*

✧

*The Encinitas baseball team, 1912.*

1911 ➤

- Cardiff resident James Frank Cullen, purchases land from Hector MacKinnon, and names his tract of land Cardiff. Encouraged by his wife, Esther, they name the streets after places in the British Isles, Cambridge, Edinburg and Oxford, to name a few. The family home is built on the corner of Oxford and Norfolk. Mr. Cullen also builds a hotel overlooking the bluff, as well as a 300-foot wooden pier south of the campgrounds and a bathhouse in 1912. The pier is later destroyed in the fierce winter storms of 1916-1917.
- Mr. Victor Kremer, music publicist/developer, names the streets after composers such as Verde, Liszt & Mozart. The lots cost $30. or $45. for a corner lot paid in six equal payments. Kremer is also credited for adding "by-the -Sea" to Cardiff.
- Cardiff Mercantile (2185 San Elijo Avenue) building is also a project of J. Frank Cullen. He builds the Cardiff Mercantile Building reminiscent of Victorian English seaside architecture. He visualized it as a hotel for artists with the first floor designed as a grocery store.

1912-15 ➤

- Cardiff Kelp Processing Plant is built 300 feet south of the present-day intersection of Kilkenny and San Elijo Ave. It processed seaweed for its many food and industrial chemicals, such as iodine for use during WWI.

*Top: Downtown Encinitas, c. 1916.*

*Middle: Coast Highway Downtown Encinitas, c. 1910. The coast highway was a dirt road until 1913 when the two-lane concrete road was constructed running from San Diego to Oceanside.*

*Bottom: The Cardiff Mercantile was designed to resemble Victorian English architecture. It was built in 1911 by J. Frank Cullen.*

*Top, left: Albert Lickert, c. 1912. This is at the corner of East Street and El Camino Del Norte in Olivenhain.*

*Top, right: Encinitas pioneer Herman Wiegand (1890-1993). The Wiegand family cultivated farmland in Olivenhain near the turn of the century.*

*Right: A couple enjoys the beach c. 1910s*

1913 ➤

- Highway 101, a two-lane concrete road, is constructed from S. D. to Oceanside.
- Cardiff-by-the-Sea School District is established.
- Cardiff Train Depot is built. Architect, Del W. Harris of San Diego designs the mission style depot. It has four rooms and is built on a cement foundation, with cement floors, plastered exterior and a tiled roof. Located slightly north and west of the Cardiff Mercantile just east of the railroad tracks. In the mid-1940s the depot is partially demolished. A section of the building, probably the ticket booth, is moved to "A" and Fifth Streets to become part of a house in Encinitas.

1914 ➤

- 1st Branch Library of San Diego County opens on October 13th in the first floor of the Cardiff Mercantile building.

## Encinitas Fun Facts
## Al's Barber Shop

In 1920, Grant Ulysses Johnston played a lucky hand of cards at the Encinitas Pool Hall and won Al's Barber shop in Encinitas. Grant had to quickly change his name to Al for all to believe it. Al's barbershop became the hottest stop during this time for gossip and "friendly" card-playing. Haircuts for men and women were only 35 cents and a shave went for 15 cents. This barbershop is now a part of the San Dieguito Heritage Museum located in Encinitas.

*Above: Proud family posing next to their home in downtown Encinitas.*

*Below: Encinitas Hotel and Clayton Drugstore shared retail space with Al's Barbershop.*

✧

*Top: The Mission School was built in 1916 in front of the 1883 one-room school. It served as an elementary school until 1936, then became the temporary San Dieguito High School. In 1953 it was moved to become part of the Self Realization Fellowship.*
*Bottom, left: Portrait of the Amos Gates Derby's wife and four daughters at the turn of the century.*

*Bottom, right: Local Encinitas family posing in their Sunday best.*

1915 ➤ • Lake Hodges Dam begins construction. Due to the flood damaged railway lines and bridges, the dam is built at the narrows of the San Dieguito River just above Rancho Santa Fe. It is completed in 1918.

1916 ➤ • Electricity comes to Encinitas via a trunk line from La Jolla.

- George's Lobster Inn (Cardiff's Restaurant Row), formerly The Beacon Inn, is built using the wood from the kelp processing plant. It has been a bar, restaurant, and gambling establishment. Hollywood stars such as Peter Lorre, Betty Grable and Jimmy Durante like the Inn and often stop on their way to San Diego.
- The Mission School is built adjacent to the original 1883 one-room schoolhouse. This serene mission-style building is located on the hill overlooking downtown at 3rd and "E" Streets. A campanile bell tower fronted the school. This new school is needed for the increasing number of students. It serves as the elementary school until 1936. The school then becomes a temporary high school until San Dieguito High is built. Some sections of the building are moved to its present location at "J" and 2nd Street in 1953 and is owned and operated by the Self Realization Fellowship, where devotees restored it.

1918 ➤ • Originally the Wenz Apartments, now known as the Danforth Building, has been in Encinitas since 1918 on the corner of First Street (Main Street Highway 101) and E Street. The southbound Greyhound bus stop was in front of the building and tickets were purchased in the building's gift shop. It included all that was needed for everyday life. The Market was open to the street, with a fruit and vegetable stand across the front, where you could buy a glass jar of milk and a loaf of bread for about 10-cents.

*Above: Wenz Apartments/Danforth Building, c. the 1930s. The Danforth Building still stands today on the northwest corner of Coast Highway and E Street.*

PHOTO COURTESY OF THE DANFORTH FAMILY.

✧

*Above: James Frank Cullen's majestic home once stood alone in Cardiff when built in 1911. It is now surrounded completely by modern homes and developments.*

*Top: Encinitas Garage on Coast Highway c. 1910s*

*Middle: Known as George's Lobster Inn (formerly the Beacon Inn) was built in 1916 with recycled wood from the closed kelp processing plant.*

*Bottom: Art Cole Hauling Hay in Olivenhain c. 1918.*

*Right and below: Life in Encinitas is booming as families discover the wonderful mild temperatures of our coastal desert climate.*

# CHAPTER 4

## THE FLOWER CAPITAL OF THE WORLD: 1920-1929

With Lake Hodges now in service, water for irrigation and home use was now readily available. Water allowed agriculture to flourish, driving the local economy. The Paul Ecke Ranch was established, bringing world famous poinsettias to the region. Downtown Encinitas started to flourish around the growth of Highway 101. This is the era of the La Paloma theater and the Boat Houses.

✧

*An aerial view of Encinitas, c. 1928.*

✧

*Top: A Williams & MacPherson Subtropical Nursery display at a flower show.*

*Bottom: The Ecke Family changed the course of Encinitas history when Paul Ecke Sr. and wife Magdalena established their poinsettia ranch along Saxony Road in 1923. This "Christmas flower" becomes a traditional addition in homes and businesses during the holiday season, now literally all over the world.*

C. 1920 ➤

- Leucadia Beach Inn (1332 N. Coast Highway 101) is designed in the popular horseshoe shape. It is now fully restored by owner Charles Marvin and continues to be the oldest continuously operating auto park style motel in California.

1922-23 ➤

- Water for the coastal areas from the completed Lake Hodges Dam comes to Leucadia allowing flowers and agriculture to flourish along with another population boom. The new San Dieguito Mutual Water Company brings water to downtown Encinitas.

1923 ➤

- Paul Ecke Poinsettia Ranch (Saxony area) is established. Paul Ecke Sr. and his family had been growing poinsettias in Hollywood since 1919. Mr. Ecke buys 40 acres at $150 an acre that previously had been the Lemuel Kincaid Ranch. Most of the world's poinsettias originated from the Paul Ecke Ranch. The Ecke family ranch house is designed by Lillian Rice and is built in 1935. Lillian Rice buildings are historic in Rancho Santa Fe. The house still remains on the property.

Above: Highway 101 in Encinitas, c. 1928. By the mid '20s downtown Encinitas was thriving with many locals starting their family business along the coast highway. Encinitas was becoming self-sufficient with services and goods being available to the active downtown district.

PHOTO COURTESY OF BETSY O'NEILL

1924 ➤

- Mid-Winter Flower Festival is started by Thomas McLaughlin in February.
- For eight years this annual event attracts crowds from all over Southern California to the downtown area along Highway 101. The 1932 depression unfortunately brings the event to a close.
- Egyptian House (959 Cornish) is built by Mr. Steele after being affected by the "Tut-mania" and the discovery of Tutankhamen's tomb in 1922. The entrance to the home is flanked by two Egyptian-style papyrus columns. Cobra goddesses with vulture wings rest above the windows, while a cobra and globe lie above the entryway. Two pilasters contain bas relief fruit, vegetable and animal shapes, along with Egyptian hieroglyphics. A similar style home is at 1239 San Dieguito.

1925 ➤

- Encinitas Hotel is built. It is noted that the lower floor is used for the 8th grade overflow. It originally had three stories, but the third floor becomes invaded by bats and is removed. This recycled wood helps build the dance hall at Moonlight Beach. When that was taken down, some lumber went to build the Boathouses.
- Dance Pavilion and Bath House is built by Aubrey Austin and deeded to the public. He also is the developer who designs and builds the La Paloma Theater.
- Dr. Charles Victor Lindsey is Encinitas' first doctor. He establishes his practice assisted by his wife, Mary, who is a nurse. From that point on he is the only doctor to deliver babies born here through 1941.

1927 ➤

- Glen Park (2149 Orinda, Cardiff-by-the-Sea) is deeded to the County of San Diego. Frank Cullen manually excavates the wash to help create the park. This property once housed the Cardiff Library in the newly built Scout Hut. Over the years the children's play area and tennis courts are added.
- Central School in Leucadia is completed (renamed Paul Ecke Central in 1986).

1928 ➤

- La Paloma Theater "The Dove" (471 So. Coast Highway 101) hosts its Grand Opening on February 11th. Costing $50,000 to build, this beautiful theater of Spanish Mission and Art Deco design, is built by Santa Monica banker, Aubrey Austin. It is one of the first theaters to show "talkies." The theater is equipped with a beautiful pipe organ and vaudeville stage. Reported as "the most exciting night in downtown Encinitas history." Over the years many performers have graced its stage. Known then as the "Broadway of the Pacific", this is referred to historically as the Aubrey Austin building as it is occupied by other businesses.
- Original 1883 One-Room Schoolhouse is sold to George Roberts for his "country home". It was moved to the corner of 4th and "H" Streets.

✧

*Right: The Aubrey Austin building, which brought to Encinitas the La Paloma Theater, has remained one of our most treasured and iconic buildings on Coast Highway. Still standing today, the building was built in 1928. This Spanish Mission-Art Deco design still attracts popular films, performances and special events.*

*Bottom: The Coast Dispatch newspaper covered everything Encinitas, literally all events including children's birthday parties. In the beginning it had a circulation of 125.*

1927-28 ➤

- The Boathouses (726 & 732 3rd Street) are built by Miles Minor Kellogg and his son, Miles Justus Kellogg. These iconic boats on 3rd Street are built with recycled lumber from the Moonlight Beach Dance Pavilion and Bathhouse that was dismantled. Miles Kellogg's Michigan family background included captains, sailors and boat builders. Each houseboat is 52 feet long and has two bedrooms, a loft, 1½ baths and a kitchen. The SS *Moonlight* and SS *Encinitas* are perched on the west side of 3rd between "F" & "G" Streets facing east.

*Above: Miles Minor Kellogg.*

*Left: Using scrap wood from the Moonlight Beach Dance pavilion Miles Justus Kellogg builds these whimsical boats on 3rd Street. In October 2019 they were placed on the National Register of Historic Places.*

✧

*Above: As life is thriving along the coast highway, Olivenhain becomes dotted with cattle ranches and dry bean farming. With wide open spaces, and very little coastal moisture, settlers relied on wells for water as they struggle to survive.*

*Below: Looking north toward the Lotus Gardens at the Self Realization Fellowship Hermitage.*

1928 ➤

- The Encinitas Sign is erected across Highway 101 south of "D" Street as the brainchild of T.J. Lewis. In 1937 it is removed to widen Highway 101.
- The Rupe Building, (137 West "D") a white art deco building, is built by Miles Kellogg. When Mr. Rupe brings his family here in 1913, he opens a small grocery store at Highway 101 and D Street. He always dreamed of a larger store. Mr. Rupe builds his new store across the street at 2nd and "D" Streets. It offers a variety of services from groceries to hardware and even a pool table. When the Great Depression hits three years later he loses everything.

1929 ➤

- The Aldrich Castle (southwest end of "H" Street) is built by Dr. Richard Aldrich, an art historian, on this one-acre site atop the 400-foot bluff. It is also referred to as "Casa San Lorenzo". Dr. Aldrich died in 1976 and developers purchase his iconic home with plans to build six two-story condominiums. They were eventually successful after a major public outcry to save the "castle" failed.
- The *Coast Dispatch* is started by Archie J. Hicks, Sr. It had a circulation of 125. In 1954, his son Archie Hicks, Jr. takes over the publishing.
- First Heritage Tree is planted on Requeza Street near Stratford Drive. It is a Cock Spar Coral and is planted by Bertrand and Margurite Butler. It is dedicated as an official Heritage Tree in 2010.

*Top: Moonlight Beach, c. the 1920s. Moonlight Beach still attracts visitors and locals alike to its gentle sandy shoreline.*

*Left: General store, c. the 1920s, Leucadia roadside park.*

## LEUCADIA

Eatonville, Eaton's Canyon, Merle, then, finally Leucadia. Named after the Greek Isle, Lefkada, this name has a litany of translations: "bright and shining isle of paradise," "sheltered paradise" or "place of refuge". All have been used in translating what the English Spiritualists meant it to be when they settled here. Leucadians have maintained the "spirit woods", this area's oldest park, Leucadia Roadside Park. The train used to stop here, too. The last known signage for this town, when it was called Merle, was at the closed train stop. Greek gods and Roman deity street names are scattered throughout Leucadia. Once there was a shooting club up in the hilly area. Wonderful roadside motels dotted the old highway 101, providing rooms for the many travelers. There was even a cafe resembling Noah's Ark, with painted plywood life-sized shapes of animals dotting the hillside. The poinsettia and flower industry put Leucadia on the map. The Ecke Ranch was ground zero for the best poinsettia operation in the world. Many other farmers in the flower industry thrived here, easily making this The Flower Capital of the World. Art studios, antique shops, shell shops and local cafes occupied most of the buildings along the highway. Today Leucadia is best known for its successful summertime Art Walk. A menagerie of "this and that" proves to be an appropriate descriptive motto that Leucadians hang on to: "Keep Leucadia Funky."

*Cardiff Beach, looking north along the then-dirt highway towards Swami's Point, Restaurant Row and San Elijo Campground now fill this landscape.*

✧

*Top: Nearly the entire community turns out for the annual Dinner Time Flower Show. This picture was taken in 1928.*

## THE MID-WINTER FLOWER FESTIVAL

The Mid-winter Flower Festival is started by Thomas McLaughlin in February of 1924. This annual event attracts flower growers and flower lovers alike from all over California. The Mid-winter Flower Show was incorporated in 1928 under California law. This event encompassed several blocks in the area of town now known as "The Lumberyard." The Great Depression caused the demise of the event in 1932.

✧

*Above: Downtown Encinitas looking west from E Street. The lot at right is the current home of the Encinitas Civic Center.*

*Right: One of the earliest known photos of the original downtown Encinitas sign. The original Encinitas sign shown here was erected in 1928. The sign was removed when Coast Highway was widened in 1937.*

# CHAPTER 5

## THE GREAT DEPRESSION AND WAR YEARS: 1930-1949

Though the region continued to expand, the Great Depression impacted the community as people looked for ways to feed the poor, led by local churches. But the growing community continued to keep an eye on the future, as San Dieguito High School opened up and Highway 101 expanded to four lanes.

Encinitas played a role in defending our Coast from attack by the Japanese, with outposts and foxholes entrenched along the coastline. But the resilience of the local citizenry wasted no time in recovering from the war, bringing electricity to Olivenhain. Encinitas' surf roots started to grow, bringing a new lifestyle and culture to the region.

*Encinitas from above.*

## Daley Double Saloon

If you are interested in stepping back in time and getting a feel for what Encinitas was like in days long past, all you have to do is pay a visit to the Daley Double Saloon at 546 First Street.

The Daley Double Saloon qualifies as one of the most unique and historical buildings in Encinitas. It's the site of Encinitas' first and oldest bar, as well as the second oldest downtown business in Encinitas (second only to the La Paloma Theater) and is a place where time appears to have stood still having changed very little over the years.

Historical records show that the building the Saloon is housed in was built in circa 1915 and that this location has always been a drinking establishment.

*Top: The art deco bar at the Daley Double Saloon in Encinitas, 1930. The famous walnut burl wood bar and cozy friendly atmosphere is still alive in this iconic bar.*

*Bottom: Before there was the Daley Double, there was the Village Rendezvous.*

1933 ➤
- Mr. Gresham's Service Station (1205 Coast Highway 101) is one of the most unique and fanciful buildings along Highway 101. He hopes to catch the eye of the many tourists that are a major component of the downtown economy from the 1920s thru the 1940s. What makes this building's architecture so unique is the Italianate style "pyramidal lip roof and blind Italian-like Arches."
- San Dieguito American Legion, Post 416 (210 West "F" Street) serves veterans, service members and the community. "It is a true testament of the dedication, commitment and hard work of several generations of active members."

1935 ➤
- Red Roof Cabins/Log Cabin Motel (1660 N. Coast Highway 101) in Leucadia are built. This motel is a true reminder of the auto court days.

1936 ➤

- The Self-Realization Hermitage (1105 2nd Street) is established. In the early 1930s while traveling by car from Los Angeles to San Diego, Paramahansa Yogananda asks his driver to pull over to the bluffs on the right to stop for a scenic picnic. He is enthralled with the majestic ocean views. Soon after Yogananda began his travels, one of his followers, James J. Lynn, purchases the property and has the hermitage built. Two years later Mr. Lynn presents this gift to Yogananda. Yogananda departs from his physical body March 1952. His dwelling has not been changed in any way. The Meditation Garden is open to the public Tuesday through Sunday. Occasionally the private areas are open for public tours.

*Above: Left to right, Muriel Kincaid, Irene Rupe, Hilda Remmele, Isabel Rupe, and Florence Kincaid.*

*Left: The Golden Lotus Temple, c. 1938. Built on the bluff within the Self Realization Fellowship grounds in 1938. Unfortunately, the temple toppled to the beach below just four years later in 1942. The tiled entryway is still prominent on the garden grounds.*

✧

*Top, left: Encinitas Central School, c. 1932.*

*Top, right: A Cardiff graduation class, c. the 1940s.*

*Bottom, right: Downtown Encinitas at the corner of "D" Street and Coast Highway. Note the old Encinitas Hotel on the top floor.*

1937 ➤

- Highway 101 is widened to a four-lane road to help accommodate the increasing traffic flow thru town, made possible by the State of California.
- The San Dieguito High School (800 Santa Fe Dr.) is dedicated on June 11th.

1939 ➤

- Rotary Club of Encinitas begins "Service Above Self" on July 12th.

The 1940s ➤

- Surfing along the entire Encinitas coastline starts becoming popular with many locations to catch that perfect wave. Surfing at Swami's is immortalized by the Beach Boys popular song, "Surfing USA." Other good surf breaks include: Stone Steps, Beacons, Pipes, Cardiff Reef, Table Tops, Stretch Mark, Brown House, Bone Yard, Little Tahiti, Old Man's, Barney's, Traps, "D" St. and Turtles.

*Top: The U.S. Navy protecting the Coast during the war.*

*Left:* "Have Yourself a Merry Little Christmas" *is a song written in 1943 by longtime Encinitas resident Hugh Martin and Ralph Blane and sung by Judy Garland in the 1944 MGM musical* Meet Me in St. Louis.

IMAGES COURTESY OF S. BOSS.

*Below: A member of the Coast Guard patrolling Encinitas.*

1941 ➤

- Black out is ordered along the Southern California coast following the bombing of Pearl Harbor. Headlights are taped revealing only a 1" slit of light. Local volunteers patrol the streets at night.

1942 ➤

- The Golden Lotus Temple on the bluffs of the Self-Realization Fellowship, topples down onto the beach below on July 21st. It had been built and dedicated just a short four years earlier on January 2, 1938.
- Japanese-American citizens, living in San Diego County on February 19th are taken to the Oceanside train depot with only one suitcase each not knowing where they are going. Due to the Civilian Exclusion Order 9060, these local citizens are transported to an internment camp in Poston, Arizona for the duration of WWII.

1946 ➤

- Electricity comes to Olivenhain.

1948 ➤

- Noah's Ark Cafe is a favorite attraction on the northwest bluff of Leucadia. It is created by George H. Herbert to resemble an ark and is flanked by several large plywood animal shapes, colorfully painted with reflectors for eyes, that are placed all over the entire hillside. Unfortunately, it is demolished in 1962.

*Top: Security check points were common during the war years along all highways.*

*Bottom: The San Dieguito High School was built in 1936/37 and dedicated on June 11. The structure for education at the high school was redesigned in 1996 as the San Dieguito Academy. It has been ranked number 74 of the 1,840 California public high schools.*

## How Encinitas Got Its Name

In 1669 Governor of Baja California Gaspar de Portola was traveling throughout the San Diego area. His plan was to build so-called presidios, where the population could learn and attend religious service. The expedition was traveling through what was later to become Encinitas. During his travels he names the area of Encinitas or the small oak tree, giving us the original name of Encina Cañada, which translated from Spanish means 'Hills of Live Oak." Over time, it became known as Encinitas, which means "Little Live Oaks."

*Top: Encinitas' first post office was co-located with the Encinitas General Merchandise Store. Cash-only.*

*Bottom: Payne Cleaners Original cleaners built in 1937. It was sold in 1946 and is still the longest continuous cleaning business in San Diego County.*

*Top: Navy sailors enjoying a day at Moonlight Beach. Note 5th Street heading north in the background.*

*Bottom: Looking south along the coast highway with the lotus towers of the Self-Realization Fellowship Hermitage and Ashram Center in the distance. The Texaco gas station was one of many service stations that dotted the coast highway.*

*Top: The Aubry Austin Building, still housing the La Paloma Theater, has been home to many businesses, including restaurants and bars. For years it was the Bank of America.*

*Bottom: The corner of E Street and Highway 101. Looking north along the coast highway in the distance is the original "Christmas Tree", adorned during the holidays by the local fire department.*

*Top: Moonlight Beach, c. the 1940s. Note the old lifeguard tower that stood until the early 1970s.*

*Middle: The Hammond Family, December 31st, 1934.*

*Bottom: View looking southeast at the very early Cardiff-By-the-Sea from the Golden Lotus Temple at the Self-Realization Fellowship .*

# CHAPTER 6

## SURF'S UP: 1950-1979

In the 1940s and 1950s, surfing took root in Encinitas. Back then, surfers surfed for love of surfing. Surfing competitively evolved in the 60s with the growth of local surf clubs like Swami's Surfing Association and Windansea Surf Club, producing world class surfers like Rusty Miller. Surfing has forever changed the culture of Encinitas.

With the opening of Interstate 5 in 1966, the region opened up like never before. People from outside the region started to discover Encinitas, leading to development changing the community forever, starting with Village Park. The population swelled. The surf culture was further celebrated by the start of the Wavecrest Woodie Meet in 1979, now in its 40th year.

*The original train station, built in 1887/88 is closed in 1969. It is bought and moved from its original location to Leucadia. The building was restored and is now the Pannikin Coffee and Tea House.*

1950ish ➤ • Jim Truax and Harry "Hodie" Zimmerman were among the first locals to take up the sport of surfing. Hodie's family opened up Zim's Diner, later to be known as the Coffee Mill, then Encinitas Café. Both Hodie and Jim were graduates of San Dieguito.

1952 ➤ • San Elijo Bluff referred for a time as the "gypsy camp" is acquired by the County of San Diego. Construction begins in 1966 and is now the popular San Elijo Campground, operated by the State of California.

*Top: Encinitas First Street from D to E Street. Over the years other building tenants have included Lou's Records, Reder Insurance, Detour Salon, a yoga studio, and a laundromat.*

PHOTO COURTESY OF KYLE THOMAS PHOTOGRAPHY

*Below: Jim Truax (front row, far left) and Hodie Zimmerman (Front row second from left)—Early Surf Pioneers.*

1953 ➤

- Second Heritage Tree (406 4th St.) is planted by Ben Danforth and sons, Peter and John, for his wife, Jane, as a Christmas present. This Norfolk Island Pine is often referred to as a Star Pine. In 1994 local citizen, Luis Ortiz, starts decorating the tree for the holidays. In 2015 the Encinitas Historical Society joined in helping to assure the community that the tree will be celebrated yearly on the first Friday of December.
- Roy's Market (1144 N. Highway 101) is built by Gerard E. Roy in October. The 3,500 square foot building, made of sturdy cinder block, serves a vital need in the Leucadia area. Mr. Roy is the butcher and also delivers groceries to shut-ins. Greyhound bus tickets are also sold at the market. It is a family operation.
- Pacific View Elementary School (608 3rd St) opens. These mid-century modern classrooms replace the Mission School. It is a functioning school until 2003. Currently (2019) it is being renovated by the Encinitas Arts Culture and Ecology Alliance (EACEA) and the Encinitas Historical Society.

✧

*Above: Luis Ortez, began decorating the Heritage Tree in 1994.*

*Below, left: Peter Danforth, one of the brothers who planted the now 100' tall Heritage Tree, working at his parent's store, the Encinitas Market, c. 1954-55.*

1954 ➤ • Hammond Family's Sunset Ranch (Saxony Road) is sold to Paul Ecke Sr. and his wife Magdelena, expanding their farming operations by 300 acres. Farmers are growing a variety of flowers throughout Encinitas such as: begonias, orchids, carnations, roses, gladioli and chrysanthemums help make this area "The Flower Capital of the World."

1956 ➤ • Leucadia Post Office (1160 North Coast Highway 101 & Phoebe) is built. Gerard Roy, owner of Roy's Market, is approached by the US Postal Service to build a specified-set-of-plans to which in-turn grant him a long-term lease to operate a new post office. Leucadia still has their own local post office.

1957 ➤ • Ruth Baird Larabee, an avid plant collector and naturalist, donates twenty-five acres of land to the County of San Diego as a park and wildlife sanctuary. Originally called El Rancho de las Flores, then Quail Park, later Quail Botanical Gardens and now officially San Diego Botanic Gardens.

• Fire Station One opens on the corner of 2nd and "C" Streets. In 1927 the citizens of Encinitas petition the county supervisors for a fire station. It is declined. Eighteen years later in 1945 they get approval. Finally, the first fire station is built and is still fully operational today.

*Top, right: The Ecke Ranch is sold to Magdalena and Paul Ecke Senior expanding their farming operation in 1945.*

*Bottom, left: The Leucadia Post Office in 1963.*

*Bottom, right: The last days of Noah's Ark before its demolition in 1962.*

## HISTORIC "OLD" ENCINITAS

Cottonwood Creek was the life blood of Encinitas. Now dedicated as an historic natural creek it is permanently recognized. This is what started our little town as the steam locomotives needed to stop to refill their supply of fresh water. Small scrub oaks, encinitos, were cut to add fuel for the engines. There were only eleven people living here, mostly Chinese rail workers, when the Hammond Family arrived and doubled the population. A school was one of their first projects. Hotels, eateries, homes and businesses sprang up quickly as the word spread that this area was indeed a good place to live. A strong sense of community support was inherent to the people of that time that can still be felt today. The railroad played a vital part as towns across America, especially in the west, were being created. It was a great time for a new life and a fresh start in the "wild west". Ranchers and farmers struggled to make a go of it. Many failed and moved on, but to this day descendants of those hardy newcomers still live in the area.

1959 ➤
- Poinsettia Heights Tract Homes changed the topography and population of Cardiff-by-the-Sea. The hills just east of I-5 soon become dotted with tract homes.

The Late 1950s ➤
- The first traffic signals were installed on Highway 101 at D and E Streets

1960 ➤
- Ada Harris School (1508 Windsor Road, Cardiff-by-the-Sea) is built in honor of their favorite teacher and principal.
- Rancho Coastal Humane Society (389 Requeza St.) is started by German immigrant Maria K. Lloyd. During WWII she witnessed the suffering of not only people but animals as well, following the Nazi invasion. Her goal is to care for the homeless animal population and to educate the public about pet over-population and responsible companion animal care.
- Population is 2,786.
- Vulcan Square Shopping Center is built on the hill above Vulcan Avenue between "D" & "E" Streets. This location is currently the Encinitas Civic Center.

*Downtown corner of Coast Highway and D Street prior to installation of Encinitas' first traffic signals.*

1961 ➤

- Elks Lodge #2243 has occupied 1393 Windsor Road, Cardiff-by-the-Sea since it was chartered on the 24th of November.
- Olivenhain Municipal Water District (1966 Olivenhain Road) is completed and water is now available to the Olivenhain Valley. OMWD President Alvin Wiegand, then 74 years old, turns the main water valve feeding an ample supply of water to the thirsty valley. Large estates and stables now cover the hillsides.
- Hansen Surfboard Shop is opened by Don Hansen in a shack in Cardiff-by-the Sea, near Cardiff reef on Highway 101.

*Above: World Champion Surfer and Encinitas local, Rusty Miller surfing at Wiamea Bay.*

1962 ➤

- The Christmas Parade begins as an annual event, which stopped in 1990 because of lack of funds. It resumes in 1994, sponsored by the City of Encinitas.The parade originally was along 2nd Street during the day. Now the Holiday Parade, is on the first Saturday of December during the early evening hours.

1963 ➤

- Caldwell's Antiques (1234 N. Hwy 101) opens by owner Charles K. Caldwell.
- Chamber of Commerce in Cardiff-by-the-Sea is officially established.
- Encinitas Hospital first opened. Founded by Dr. Charles Clark, Dr. Ronald Summers, Dr. Dwight Cook and Herman "Pop" Wiegand.
- Rusty Miller is crowned world surfing champion by the World Surfing Federation. Rusty was a local surfing favorite and lifeguard at Moonlight Beach in the 1960s. Rusty moved to Encinitas at age 5 and started surfing at age 10.

1965 ➤

- Besta Wan Pizza House (148 Aberdeen) is opened by the Corder Family on March 12th. It is still there today with parking and a "play" area in front.
- Pacific View Elementary School Expands to 2.8 acres when the school district purchases two houses on the south side for a larger playground area.
- Lake Val Sereno is purchased and constructs the ill-fated "lake front homes".

- Local Encinitas surfer, Danielle Corn, was a last-minute replacement to join Mike Doyle to compete in the Makaha World Tandem Surfing Championship on Oahu, Hawaii. With limited time to practice, Danielle and Mike went on to win the competition..

1966 ➤
- Interstate I-5 Freeway is completed.
- Boys & Girls Club of San Dieguito (1221 Encinitas Blvd) opens in Encinitas in a donated temporary building.
- Encinitas Branch Library (540 Cornish Dr.), proudly opens its modern 4,100 square foot round facility.

1967 ➤
- Snow on December 13th falls in Encinitas. Prior reported snowfall was in 1933.

*Top, left: Danielle Corn and Mike Doyle at the World Tandem Surfing Championship in Oahu, Hawaii.*

*Bottom left: The Encinitas Hospital at Santa Fe ribbon-cutting Ceremony, October 24, 1963. From Left to right: Dr. Hughes, Dr. Cook, Dr. Clark, and Dr. Summers.*

*Bottom, right: The Freeway 5 ribbon cutting ceremony, June 21, 1966.*

**June 21. 1966**

*Above: Local Leucadians gather to install the Leucadia welcome sign.*

COURTESY OF THE CALDWELL FAMILY.

*Right: Moonlight Beach, c. the 1960s. Note the old boardwalk connecting the beach south to north.*

1969 ➤

- VG Donut & Bakery (106 Aberdeen) opens in the new strip mall in Cardiff-by-the-Sea. Still owned by the Metee family, this landmark business is now an icon, providing the community with "very good" donuts.
- YMCA (200 Saxony Road) begins construction on the first five-acre plot of land donated from the Ecke Family. In 1988 the Ecke Family donates additional land for a total of 20 acres to become the "Magdelena Ecke Family YMCA".

c. 1970 ➤

- Village Park started developing tract homes, apartments and duplexes in the eastern portion of Encinitas, replacing the area that was our city dump and a prosperous bee keeping business. The last phase was completed in c.1985.

1970 ➤

- Encinitas Train Station/Pannikin Coffee & Tea House (510 N. Coast Highway 101) is started in the original train station building which was closed in 1969. The building is sold for $1 but has to be moved to its present location costing $35,000. John Henderson was the architect that restored the building. It is initially an arts and crafts shop. Today it remains a popular local gathering spot.
- Quail Park (Quail Gardens Rd.) opens the Larabee land to the public by the County of San Diego. It quickly became a popular tourist attraction.
- Cap'n Kenos (158 North Highway 101) was originally built in 1929. This building has morphed over time and has historically been the Kolb's Drive-In, owned and operated by Aubrey Austin, who built the La Paloma Theater complex and Moonlight Beach bathhouse. It has also been the Vienna Villa, Shamrock Cafe and El Rancho Restaurant. Gerry Sova buys the business and for only a few months calls it "The Green Apple." Gerry runs the bar and restaurant as well as cooks and serves tables. Today this landmark local treasure is still "hoppin."
- Population is 5,375.

*Above: "Locals" enjoy a winter day at Moonlight Beach. Note the playground looking south.*

*Below: Young local surfers descend the stairs at Swamis Point to catch a few waves.*

JUNE | JULY 2015

encinitas

EAT DRINK ARTS PEOPLE PLACES magazine

✧

*Encinitas Magazine featured article Stone Steps Surf Contest 1975, by photojournalist and Encinitas local Kyle Thomas.*

COURTESY OF ENCINITAS MAGAZINE EDITOR IN CHIEF CHRIS COTE

# Stone Steps Invitational Surfing Contest

If you grew up and lived in Encinitas from 1967 to 1979, the Stone Steps Invitational Surfing Contest was an event that you just didn't want to miss.

It was the Woodstock of Encinitas—Music—Beer—Big crowds—There was just nothing else like it.

If you hadn't seen a local Encinitas friend or two for a while, you were guaranteed to run across them here, on this day. If you didn't, it was because they were either in the hospital, in jail, or had died.

The contest was a huge, challenging event to organize and set up. It was not sanctioned by the State of California, which had jurisdiction over beach access, making it illegal, and therefore had to be set up in secret under the cover-of-darkness the night before the event.

Everything had to be walked down the stairs—all 100 kegs of beer. The band stage had to be carried down, along with the speakers and everything else it would take to put on the party.

The rules of the contest were simple: When the starting gun goes off signaling the beginning of your heat, you have to guzzle a resin bucket full of beer—then go surf. The winner of the heat goes on to drink more beer and surf more heats, until finally, from the last group standing—and that can still surf, a "winner" is selected.

Encinitas historian and Stone Steps contest organizer John Peugh sums it up quite nicely when he says, "This thing was started purely to have fun. It wasn't about who won, or if it was, you wouldn't be drinking all that beer before you went out into the water!"

*Top, right and bottom: The Stone Steps surfing contest gained popularity in the 1960s as interest in surfing exploded.*

1975 - PHOTO BY KYLE THOMAS

*Top: Moonlight Beach looking north. Note the playground equipment and picnic pavilion at left.*

*Right: Moonlight Beach, c. the 1960s looking south. Note the Lifeguard Tower along the Boardwalk. Local surfing legend Rusty Miller served as a lifeguard here in the mid-1960s.*

OPPOSITE PAGE PHOTOS COURTESY OF LEROY GRANNIS.

1975 ➤
- La Asociacion de Charros de Encinitas is formally chartered. The event celebrated life on the great land ranchos before California became a state.

1976 ➤
- Mira Costa Community College (3333 Manchester Ave.) purchases 42 acres for the Cardiff-by-the-Sea campus that was dedicated in 1988.

1977 ➤
- La Especial Norte (664 N. Highway 101) is opened by Angel & Matilde Salazar.

1979 ➤
- Greek Orthodox Church (3459 Manchester Ave.) is built but not consecrated until June 2001. Known as "the Church with the Shining Cross" as the sun adds a serendipitous cross that shines a reflection on the gilded dome.
- Wavecrest Woodie Meet has their first gathering in the parking lot at Moonlight Beach. San Diego Woodies continue to meet in September every year at 4th and "B" Streets. September 2019 celebrates their 40th year.

## LINDA BENSON

The life of the surfer girl who grew up on Dewitt Street in Encinitas, Linda Benson, has been remarkable. In 1959 at age 15, Linda was not only the first woman to win the first national surfing contest held in the US at the West Coast Championships in Huntington Beach, but is also credited to be the first woman to ride the legendary big waves of Waimea Bay. That same year she became the youngest contestant ever, to enter the International Surfing Contest at Makaha, which she won.

Linda continued competing for 10 years winning the women's 1960 and 1961 West Coast Championships and the women's 1964 and 1968 US Surfing Championships.

Winning over twenty first-place surfing titles from 1959 to 1969, Linda was discovered by Hollywood and acted as Annette Funicello's

*Article reprint courtesy of Encinitas Magazine Editor in Chief Chris Cote.*

RIGHT PHOTO COURTESY OF WAX PHOTOS.

BOTTOM, LEFT PHOTO COURTESY OF LINDA BENSON.

BOTTOM, RIGHT PHOTO COURTESY OF KYLE THOMAS PHOTOGRAPHY..

surfing double in the "Beach Party" films, and as Deborah Walley's surfing double in *Gidget Goes Hawaiian*. She appeared in Bud Browne and John Severson films, and she was in the first *Surfer Magazine* in 1960. She was also the first woman to grace the cover of a surfing magazine, *Surf Guide 1963*.

Reflecting back, Linda remembers getting her first surfboard. "When I was eleven, there was a water-soaked balsa board for sale for $20.00 and my Dad let me get it."

"John Elwell was one of the lifeguards at Moonlight Beach," Linda recounts. "He really took a lot of us under his wing—Rusty Miller, my friend Nikki and myself."

"Our parents drove us on the weekends to Swamis. We walked to the beach in the summertime. We could be down there as long as the lifeguards were there. So grateful to have parents that let us do that. They trusted me. When wintertime came then everyone went to Swamis. "So the weekends, my parents and Nicky's parents took turns driving us to Swami's and that's where we were all weekend."

If you ask Linda today what her philosophy on life is, she'll tell you, "Keep on paddling!"

# CHAPTER 7

## INCORPORATED! ENCINITAS GROWS UP: 1980-1999

Encinitas and the surrounding area continue to grow. By the vote of the people, Cardiff, Historic Encinitas, New Encinitas, Leucadia and Olivenhain become one city, leading to the community incorporating and exercising self-governance. As our community rapidly moves ahead the Encinitas Historical Society is formed, followed by the San Dieguito Heritage Museum to collect and save our history. San Elijo Lagoon Conservancy is created to protect this vital area as one of the last remaining California coastal wetlands. Downtown Encinitas Mainstreet Association fulfills the requirements to join the National Mainstreet Association to assist in advancing our historical 101 business district. Later, Leucadia and Cardiff are also accepted. Cottonwood Creek is recognized on the National Registry of Historic Places, along with Indian Head Canyon.

*Encinitas aerial photo looking north from Swamis Point.*

✧

*Above: The San Dieguito Heritage Museum sets its final roots on Quail Gardens Drive. Established in 1988, it has been housed in many locations. This locally focused museum collects and displays objects and buildings from Encinitas' past.*

*Below: San Elijo Lagoon on a classic misty morning looking southeast.*

PHOTO COURTESY OF MORGAN MALLORY.

1980 ➤

- Value Fair & Vons Shopping Center (c.1960 at 2000 block of San Elijo Ave). in Cardiff-by-the-Sea is demolished making way for the new Cardiff Town Center.
- Friends of the Encinitas Library is founded. The Friends play a vital role in raising money and advocating the need for a larger facility.
- Teten House (450 Quail Gardens Dr.) is moved by the San Dieguito Heritage Museum to its permanent location. Extensive rehabilitation and restoration efforts commence. It is now complete and open to the public on the museum property.
- Encinitas Historical Society (390 West F St.) originally the Leucadia-Encinitas Historical Society is incorporated. "The mission of the Encinitas Historical Society is to collect, archive and preserve the many documents, photos, videos and oral histories that shape our heritage, and to maintain the health and integrity of the oldest building in the City, the 1883 One-Room Schoolhouse."
- Population is 36,550.

1982 ➤ • The Lumberyard Center (700-1000 blocks of Coast Highway 101) in downtown Encinitas is built using a railroad-style architecture.

• Downtown Encinitas Merchants Association is formed to aid and promote businesses along Coast Highway 101 in downtown Encinitas. In 1988 the organization is granted the National Mainstreet Association status. It later becomes known as Downtown Encinitas Mainstreet Association "DEMA." Currently nicknamed as E-101, they also manage the street fairs twice a year.

1983 ➤ • San Elijo Lagoon Conservancy (2710 Manchester Ave.) started by a small group of concerned citizens to save the lagoon, is formally dedicated to the public. This important lagoon is one of the few remaining coastal wetlands in the state as it is the terminus of the Escondido Creek. The lagoon is 915 acres with over seven miles of hiking trails and a 5,600-square-foot Nature Center. Prior to the 1970s, developers were proposing to replace the lagoon with condominiums, a marina and a water park. It is now jointly managed by the San Diego County Department of Parks and Recreation, the Department of Fish and Wildlife and supported by the San Elijo Lagoon Conservancy who bought the land in 2012.

✧

*Above: Citizens of all five districts vote to create one city: Encinitas, on October 1, 1986. The first Encinitas City Council members to be elected are, (from left to right): Greg Luke, Marjorie Gaines, Rick Shea, Gerald Steel, and Anne Omsted.*

*Bottom, right: The Lumberyard Shopping Center was built in 1982 in a railroad-style architecture as this area was literally the lumber yard during the early boom years, as well as the site of the Mid-Winter Flower Festival.*

*Top: The 1883 schoolhouse nearing its final resting place on West F Street. The one-room schoolhouse is moved back to close to it's original site in 1983, only 100 feet from where it first served the community. Saved by the Encinitas Historical Society, the Encinitas Elementary School board approves it's location on the south/west corner of the active Pacific View Elementary School.*

*Bottom: The original wooden railroad trestles that ran between Cardiff-by-the-Sea and Solana Beach over the San Elijo Lagoon. The new double tracking project was completed in 2021.*

PHOTO COURTESY OF MORGAN MALLORY.

- The Encinitas Historical Society works quickly to save the original 1883 one-room schoolhouse from demolition. Bud Fisher offers the building to the Society. The Society is granted a small leased section in the southwest corner of the Pacific View Elementary School property at 390 West F Street. The schoolhouse is bought on April 13th for $1 but costs $2,300 to move.

1984 ➤

- Quail Park (Quail Gardens Dr.) changes its name to Quail Botanical Garden.
- Friends of the Cardiff Library is formed.

1986 ➤

- The City of Encinitas on October 1st is created when five small uniquely individual communities become a city. Three prospective names were on the ballot; Rancho San Elijo, San Dieguito and of course Encinitas. Community activist, Marjorie Gaines, is appointed first mayor of the newly incorporated city. The Civic Center it is now permanently located at 505 South Vulcan Ave.

## California Surf Museum Gets its Start in Encinitas

Stuart Resor, an Encinitas resident and surfer, says…"I got the idea to start preserving our surf history when I saw Woody Ekstrom walking down the beach at Grand View in Leucadia. It suddenly seemed to me that the early days of surfing were slipping behind us and if he and others were interested, we could display old surfboards and photographs for future generations to see."

In February 1986, after an article appeared in The Coast Dispatch and The Citizen newspapers, several interested people came together at George's Restaurant on Coast Highway in Encinitas to discuss forming a surf museum.

The dozen or so people who showed up for that first meeting became the founding board, a mix of men and women, surfers and non-surfers, connected by an avid interest in surfing and a desire to collect its history for the enjoyment of generations to come. The founding members were Mike Cates, June Chocheles, Don Fine, Steve George, Kevin Kinnear, Parry Payne, Stuart Resor, Jane Schmauss, Ian Urquhart, and Catherine Woolsey.

*The most famous exhibit at the museum is the story of Bethany Hamilton losing her left arm to a tiger shark while surfing at Tunnels Beach on Kauai, how she survived that attack to not only recover from the incident, but returned to competitive surfing—and she continues to do well in surfing contests around the world. Her story and her positive outlook on life have caused her to be in demand as a motivational speaker. The exhibit features the surfboard Bethany was riding on that fateful Halloween day in 2003, the bathing suit she was wearing, featured in the documentary* Heart of a Soul Surfer.

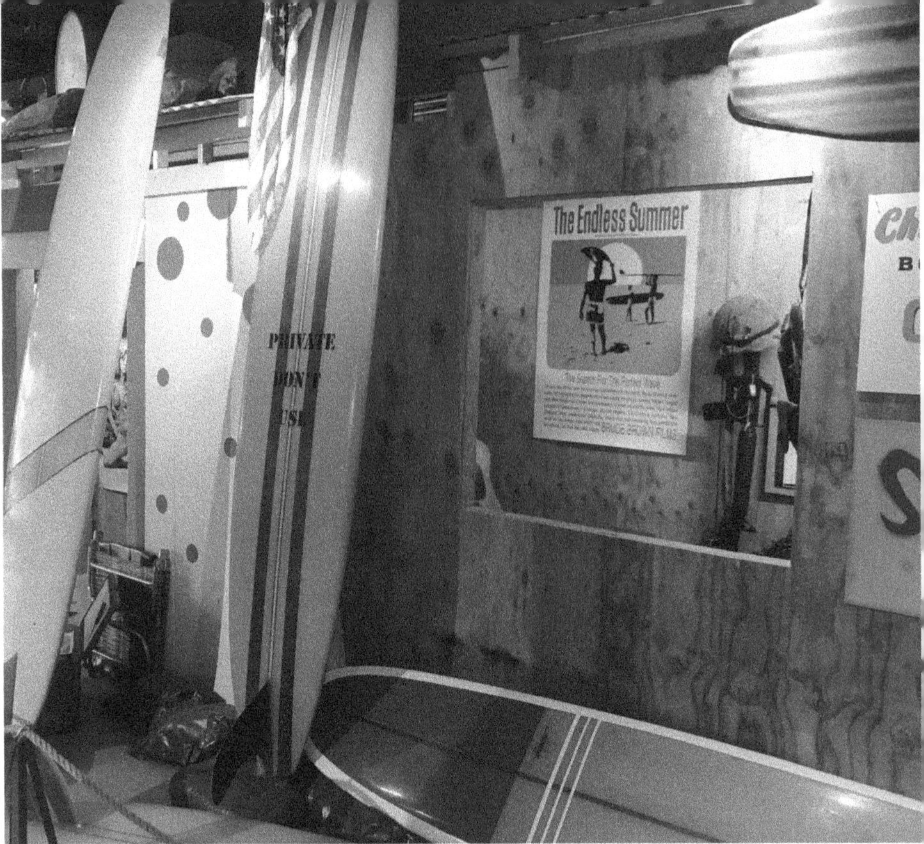

The California Surf Museum took shape as a small display of surfboards and surf collectibles at George's Restaurant, owned by Jane Schmauss, in 1986. The restaurant was open 7 days a week and had a little corner alcove dedicated to promoting the museum concept. The Board voted to use the name "California Surf Museum" after discussing the merits of the Encinitas Surf Museum, the North County Surfing Museum, and numerous other names, believing that the broader term would one day link to a string of museums up and down the coast, such as the "California Surf Museum, Ventura," and the like.

After many months of organizing and putting together a logo design contest (won by Ed Nava), Encinitas businessman Paul Rotsheck offered the fledgling California Surf Museum free space in his newly built Moonlight Plaza, on the corner of Encinitas Boulevard and the Coast Highway. CSM mounted its first exhibit, "Surfing: Trestles to Tourmaline," on August 13, 1988, with a grand opening September 28, 1988.

The surf museum found its new home in Oceanside, California, in 1996.

1987 ➤

- Indian Head Canyon (north Saxony) is saved from developers when several dedicated citizens gather to support the purchase of these 60 acres. The goal is to save this lush canyon as open space and stop the planned tract of 300 homes. After a long eleven-year struggle, the city, along with the assistance of the California Conservation Corp, joins to officially declare it public land in 1998.
- Coast News started in the garage of Jim Kydd on September 17. It is currently in publication, with Chris Kydd, Jim's son, as the current publisher.

1988 ➤

- Downtown Encinitas Mainstreet Association (DEMA) is officially awarded membership into the National Mainstreet Association.
- The San Dieguito Heritage Museum is created. This locally focused museum collects and displays objects that represent everyday life of the pioneers and their families. Interactive exhibits and representatives of different cultures make the past come alive in and around these historic buildings. The museum is now permanently located on 1.2 acres on Quail Gardens Drive. The property is leased from the City of Encinitas for $1 per year for fifty-five years.

*These iconic boathouses built by Miles Justus Kellogg in 1927/28 were placed on the National Register of Historic Places in October 2019.*

*Above: Encinitas and Amakusa, Japan, have been sister cities since 1988.*

*Below, left: Coast Highway between D and E Streets with the old Detour Salon, Beach & Town Liquor, and Flashbacks*

*Below, right: Encinitas Child located near the Cottonwood Creek overlook. This bronze statue welcomes visitors to the downtown area.*

1988 ➤

- A Sister City relationship with Hondo, Japan, Kumamoto prefecture was officially established. In this area of Japan, the government combines several small communities (like Encinitas in 1986) and is renamed Amakusa on March 27, 2006. Many cultural exchanges have taken place with students, fire fighters, medical personnel and government officials. There is a mile marker at the base of 2rd and "B" Streets that show the miles to our Sister City as 6,129 miles.
- Swami's Beach sign is erected at Swami's Point by the Swami's Surf Association.

1989 ➤

- Moonlight Beach supervision and maintenance is taken over by the City of Encinitas from the state. Local lifeguards are hired.

1990 ➤

- Population is 55,386.

1991 ➤ • Cottonwood Creek (Hwy 101 and "B" Street) is recognized and placed on the National Registry of Historic Places on August 5th spearheaded by Ida Lou Coley. Cottonwood Creek is the key reason Encinitas became a town. It was the first town between National City and Oceanside to spring up along the western section of San Diego county. From 1881 to 1920, Cottonwood Creek served not only as the main water source for the growing community but provided the much-needed water to run the steam locomotives.

• Vulcan Square Shopping Center, (505 S. Vulcan Ave) built in 1960 is sold to the City of Encinitas to remodel as the new Encinitas Civic Center (City Hall).

1992 ➤ • North County Transit District (NCTD) buys the Santa Fe Rail Line from San Diego to Oceanside.

1993 ➤ • The Olivenhain Town Hall (423 Rancho Santa Fe Rd.) is placed on the National Register of Historic Places.

1994 ➤ • The Encinitas Heritage Tree is adorned for the Holiday Season for the first time by Luis Ortiz. In 2011, the tree was officially protected as a Heritage Tree by the City of Encinitas. In 2015, the Encinitas Historical Society became the official sponsor of the lighting ceremony. Luis continues leading the lighting of the tree to this day.

*Below, left:Veteran's Memorial Cottonwood Creek Park.*

*Below, right: An Egret in the San Elijo Lagoon*

PHOTO COURTESY OF MORGAN MALLORY.

Top: *San Diego Botanic Garden. Quail Botanical Gardens changed it's name to San Diego Botanic Gardens in 2009. It is one of the worlds best known established gardens providing cuttings, plants and seeds to other gardens throughout the world.*

*Bottom: The Leucadia Welcome Sign. Members of the Leucadia Town Council spruce up and replant the area around the Welcome Sign at the north entrance along the coast highway.*

1995 ➤

- Coaster Commuter Train has its inaugural run from Oceanside to the downtown San Diego Santa Fe Depot on February 27th.

1997 ➤

- Machado Surf Classic has its inaugural surf competition in late summer at Cardiff State Beach and is sponsored by the Cardiff Chamber of Commerce. In 2002 the event name is changed to Hansen/Machado Surf Professional Event, sanctioned by the Association of Surfing Professionals (ASP).
- La Bajada Bridge over the Escondido Creek connecting Encinitas to Rancho Santa Fe officially opened. This area consistently flooded during the rainy season.
- 1883 One-Room Schoolhouse (390 West "F") in December is now fully restored and open to the public. Total cost, along with many volunteer hours, is $17,000.
- Carpentier Parkway (the "front garden" between Birmingham & Chesterfield) is named after Orville & Jessica Carpentier. A statue is erected in the image of the late Wayne Holden, a Cardiff-by-the-Sea community activist.

1998 ➤

- Indian Head Canyon along the north end of Saxony Road in Leucadia, with the addition of donated land from Magdalena Ecke Park, is officially declared public land encompassing over 90 acres.
- 101 Artists' Colony is formed as a co-op artists gallery by James Durfey, Nansy Phleger and Maria Festa. It has been in several locations in Encinitas with studios, performance stage, galleries and a coffee bar. It is supported solely by local artists.
- Encinitas Ranch Golf Course, owned by the City of Encinitas, is opened to the public on March 1st. Rated a Champion Golf Course with 18-holes on 175 acres.

1999 ➤

- Cullen School Bell is dedicated at the Cardiff Elementary School on October 23rd. The bell was purchased in Santa Ana for $20.00 and has a manufactured date of 1828. It is re-dedicated again in 2003 during the refurbished Cardiff School District's 90th anniversary.
- Full Moon Poets was formed by Danny Salzhandler for the laid-back poetry circle called a "read around." It has grown to include a Summer Slam and a Winter Slam during the full moons and held at the historic La Paloma Theater.

*Below: Olympic torch run through Encinitas on April 28, 1996. Local dignitaries help run the Olympic Torch through Encinitas on it's way to the summer games in Atlanta, Georgia. The world games of the XXVI Olympiad was also known as the Centennial Olympic Games.*

PHOTO COURTESY OF KYLE THOMAS.

## CARDIFF-BY-THE-SEA

Cardiff had an early start and a fascinating history. Streets were named after the British Isles, followed by more streets named after classical music composers. Cardiff, was located on a beautiful part of the California coastline. One of its first settlers erected a two-story building reminiscent of a Victorian English seaside manor. The building provided an artists' studio on the second floor. During that same year "by-the-Sea" was added to its name. Remnants of Cardiff's only industry can still be seen during low tide where a kelp processing plant operated. The pier, which was built near the mouth of the lagoon, has long since washed away. The main cement floor of Cardiff's one and only train station is all that remains of the mission style depot. Restaurant Row was known to host many a celebrity traveling back and forth from Hollywood to Del Mar and Mexico. Japanese farmers' crops covered the hills just east of town. The San Elijo lagoon was slowly choking. The mouth was opened occasionally by a farmer with a plow. Cardiff-by-the-Sea later changed to a new personality - surfing. It is where Don Hansen opened his first shop; where "the kook" put Cardiff-by-the-Sea on the international map; where surfing contests and beach fairs rocked the coast. Double tracking, the lagoon improvements, Harbaugh Trails and the Living Shoreline Project may have changed the scene, but not the heart: the pull is real and it is the soul of Cardiff-by-the-Sea.

*Above: Cardiff-by-the-Sea looking north toward Swamis Point. A typical beautiful summer day looking north along the Cardiff coastline.*

*Right: Local large mural artist Kevin Anderson paints a new San Dieguito Academy mural on the north wall of the main building. Many of his murals can be seen throughout Encinitas and San Diego County.*

*The Downtown Encinitas 101 Mainstreet Association contracted several local artists to enhance the alleys and back buildings of many businesses along Coast Highway.*

PHOTOGRAPH BY DAPHNE FLETCHER.

# Chapter 8

## The New Millennium: 2000-Present

Encinitas' culture, rooted in surfing and the arts, advances. The Arts Alive Banner program launches along Coast Highway 101; the first Switchfoot Bro-Am and Beach Fest is held at Moonlight Beach; Dog Days of Summer begins in Cardiff; the "Kook" is dedicated in Cardiff; the Encinitas Child sculpture is dedicated near Cottonwood Creek and the Surfing Madonna Mosaic appears to everyone's delight; the first community garden is constructed; we elect our first mayor; create our new Encinitas Community park and focus on beach erosion, protection and expanded access to hiking trails and marine safety.

2000 ➤

- Arts Alive Banner Exhibit launches on Highway 101 in downtown Encinitas. This very successful and popular program is spearheaded by local artist, sculptor and welder Danny Salzhandler, his wife Norma and the 101 Artists' Colony.
- Encinitas Sign on October 7th , duplicated from the original 1928 sign across D Street at 101. It is rebuilt using the original design to celebrate the millennial. It was first hung on cables but a storm two weeks later almost brought it down. Later a solid steel support frame was installed. I true icon for our coastal town.
- Population is 58,014.
- Encinitas Community/Senior Center is completed on Oakcrest Park Drive.

2002 ➤

- Downtown Streetscape Project has its Ribbon Cutting in June.

2003 ➤

- Cardiff Library opens its new 5,977 sq. ft. "green" facility, (1st in the county) on the corner of Newcastle & Liverpool on March 22nd.
- The Pacific View Elementary School is closed at the end of the school year.
- Leucadia-Encinitas Mainstreet Organization is awarded National Mainstreet status, becoming Leucadia 101 (L 101).

2004 ➤

- Cottonwood Creek Park has its ribbon cutting celebration June 14th. This 8.2-acre park is located on the northeast corner of Encinitas Blvd. and Vulcan Ave.
- Switchfoot Bro-Am and Beach Fest is started by local surf legend Rob Machado and local, world famous Christian musicians, Switchfoot. This event includes surf contests, live music and much more always in the month of June.
- Dog Days of Summer has their first event in the parking lot of Headline Graphics in Cardiff-by-the-Sea. In 2016 this popular event is moved to the new Encinitas Community Park. This is the largest dog-centric event in San Diego County.
- Poet Laureate Trish Dugger is recognized officially on January 12 by the City.

*The Wavecrest Woodie Meet has their first gathering in the parking lot at Moonlight Beach. September 2019 was the 40th consecutive year drawing cars and woodie enthusiasts from all over the country to display and sell these iconic cars.*

COURTESY OF JENNIFER NELSON

Above: *Moonlight Beach.*

PHOTOGRAPH BY DAPHNE FLETCHER.

*Left: Switchfoot Bro-Am and Beach Fest, started by local Rob Machado, features the Christian band Switchfoot. Thousands of fans pack Moonlight Beach, c. 2018.*

PHOTOGRAPH BY DAPHNE FLETCHER.

2007 ➤

- Magic Carpet Ride or Cardiff "Kook" is the creation of Matthew Antichevich. Since its debut, local surfers have deemed it a "kook", which refers to a first time or beginner surfer. This wonderful statue, along the west side of Highway 101 across from Chesterfield Drive, becomes an unlikely attraction when a 15-foot-tall papier mache shark appears to devour the "Kook." Costumes and props are now a common sight. Cleverly outfitted for birthdays, graduations, special events and political satire, the "Kook" has worn it all. The "Kook" is featured in many publications around the world, including the front page of the *Wall Street Journal*.

2008 ➤

- Encinitas Preservation Association (EPA) is formed and closes escrow on the iconic Boathouses for $1.55 million in May. It is touted as a "public trust of preservation" by the Encinitas Historical Society and Downtown Encinitas Mainstreet Association. The City of Encinitas use a developer's fee of $631,538 as the down payment designated as affordable housing. Plans commence to place these iconic boats on the National Register of Historic Places. The E Clampus Vitus organization partners with EPA to assist with the historical bronze plaque.

Top: A few banners created by local artists along Coast Highway promoted by the Artist Colony's "Arts Alive" community program.

Above: Swami's Beach & Park.

COURTESY OF DAPHNE FLETCHER

Right: "Dog Days of Summer", first held in a parking lot in Cardiff in 2005. It expanded to Encinitas Community Park, holding various events like the dog/owner look-alike contest.

- Encinitas Library (540 Cornish Dr.) has occupied several locations, including one on the corner of "D" Street in the Rupe Building during the 1940s into the mid-1950s. Manuel Oncina Architects, Inc. are contracted to design a new state-of-the-art facility, financed by the City of Encinitas. On February 23rd the \$20-million-dollar, 27,798-square-foot library opens. This facility includes a 2,000-square-foot Community Room, 537-square-foot Special Collections Room, an informal Literary Lab with 15 computer workstations for group instruction and three group study rooms. A reading deck along the west side, a Friends of the Library bookstore and an entry coffee cart are part of the main space. Civic Art shows are included as part of the library design, with local artists and performers playing an integral part of the library's design.

2008 ➤
- "Encinitas Child" is seated on the retaining wall on the west side on Highway 101 between Encinitas Blvd. and D Street welcoming visitors to the downtown area. This beautiful bronze sculpture is created by local and nationally renowned sculptor Manuelita Brown. To celebrate its 20th anniversary the Downtown Encinitas Mainstreet Association (DEMA) installs this public art piece.

2010 ➤
- Pacific Station development opens on Highway 101. Whole Foods is the anchor business. Apartments are on the 2nd floor with underground parking for 250 cars.
- Population is 59,519.

2011 ➤
- Surfing Madonna Mosaic literally appeared overnight under the north side of the railroad bridge on Encinitas Blvd. Disguised as construction workers, Mark Patterson and friend Bob Nichols clandestinely install the 10-foot square, glass mosaic art piece on an early April morning. When threatened with demolition, Patterson steps forward to save his creation. He is fined $500 and has to pay $6,000 to have it removed. In 2013 the mosaic finds its permanent home on the outside north facing wall of the Leucadia Pizzeria on Encinitas Blvd & 101. In 2019 artist Kevin Anderson paints an underwater scene below the mosaic.

*Above, left: Coaster in Cardiff.*

PHOTOGRAPH BY NEAL GLASGOW

*Above, right: Swami's Beach gets a second Tiki statue, joining the first carved by Tim Richards in 2011 from an 80 yr. old Torrey Pine that fell victim to bark beetle infestation.*

COURTESY OF DAPHNE FLETCHER

*Below, left: Downtown Encinitas.*

PHOTOGRAPH BY DAPHNE FLETCHER

*Below, right: Swami's Surf Memorial at Swami's Beach.*

COURTESY OF DAPHNE FLETCHER

✧

*Top, left: Santa Fe Drive railroad undercrossing at Swami's Beach Park officially opens.*

COURTESY OF DAPHNE FLETCHER

*Top, right: The lotus towers of the SRF Hermitage and Ashram Center.*

COURTESY OF DAPHNE FLETCHER

2012 ➤

- "The Ranch" (441 Saxony Rd.) formerly known as the Ecke RanchFloriculture business, sells its property to the Leichtag Foundation. This 67 ½-acre ranch has a total of 850,000 square feet of green houses.
- First electrical vehicle charging station is put into use in July at the north end of parking lot B just east of 101 at D Street and Vulcan Avenue.

2013 ➤

- Santa Fe Drive Pedestrian under-crossing is officially opened on February 27th connecting South Vulcan to Highway 101 allowing easy access to Swami's Beach.

2014 ➤

- Plastic Ban on single-use plastic bags is passed by the City of Encinitas.
- First Elected Mayor of Encinitas, Kristin Gaspar, is voted in on November 7th. Previously the elected council members rotated the position on a yearly basis.
- Welcome sign is dedicated at the south entry near the under crossing on Highway 101 into downtown Encinitas. Bob Partlow and Terry Weaver design and create this sand blasted 8X10 foot redwood sign. This is a project of the Downtown Encinitas Mainstreet Association (DEMA).
- Pacific View Property is purchased by the City of Encinitas with a $10 million bond. The old elementary school (closed since 2003) had been scheduled for auction. The total bond package is $13 million, with three million earmarked for building the new lifeguard tower at Moonlight Beach.
- Leichtag Foundation (441 Saxony Rd) joins six other Encinitas entities to sign a "Memorandum of Understanding" (MOU) in April. They include The Encinitas Union School District, the Magdalena Ecke Family YMCA, The San Diego Botanic Gardens, The San Dieguito Heritage Museum, Seacrest Village Retirement Community, along with the Leichtag Foundation "...to develop educational, experimental learning and multi-generational programs around the nexus of agriculture, horticulture, nutrition, science, sustainability, community building and the local history and agricultural traditions of Encinitas."

- Cardiff-by-the-Sea Mainstreet Association, formerly Cardiff Chamber of Commerce, is identified as an official main street organization (C 101).

2015 ➤

- Encinitas Community Park (425 Santa Fe Dr.) is officially opened on January 10th. Formerly the greenhouse floral business of Robert Hall, he sells the property to the City of Encinitas in 2000 for $17,000,000. The total cost over the next 15 years totals $42,750,000. This 44-acre park boasts a 13,000-square-foot renowned skate park, kids play areas, two acres for the Maggie Houlihan Memorial Dog Park, athletic fields and lots of open green spaces.
- Encinitas Arts, Culture and Ecology Alliance (EACEA) enters into negotiations with the City of Encinitas to transform the closed 2.8-acre Pacific View Elementary School into a viable arts center. Rehabilitation commences in a right-of-entry lease situation while the long-term lease requirements are finalized.
- Coastal Roots Farm (441 Saxony Road), dedicated on September 30 and located on the Leichtag Property, begin their certified organic farming operation. It is a non-profit educational community farm where growing organic vegetables "nourish connections—to ourselves, our neighbors and the land", inspired by Jewish wisdom. Fresh organic produce is sold at their Farm Stand as a pay-what-you-can system to offer healthy, organically grown produce for all.
- Organic Fruit Grove is dedicated at Glen Park in Cardiff-by-the-Sea on October 3rd, inspired by Cardiff resident and former mayor Teresa Arballo Barth. This is an organically managed city park setting the tone for healthy organic gardening.
- Friends of the Arts received non-profit status on November 27. Created in 2014, the mission of EFA is to partner with the City of Encinitas by "fund raising and advocating for art in Encinitas and city owned art venues promoting all art forms".

*Below: Encinitas Sign on Coast Highway 101. The Downtown Encinitas Mainstreet Association contracts Bob Partlow and Terry Weaver in 2014 to create this Welcome sign on the south end of the business district entering the coast highway.*

COURTESY OF DAPHNE FLETCHER

✧

*Above: Swami's Pumpkins, Every year the SRF plants their fields with pumpkins to carve for Halloween.*

PHOTO COURTESY OF KYLE THOMAS.

2016 ➤

- Encinitas Community Garden (Quail Gardens Drive) ribbon cutting is in October. Community members rally to create this garden on Quail Gardens Drive in the undeveloped Encinitas Elementary School site. A total of eighty-nine raised beds are constructed along with eighty fruit trees. Gordon Smith is the "slow foods" advocate who started the process to make this garden a reality.

2017 ➤

- Cannabis (marijuana)for recreational consumption is approved by statewide vote.

2018 ➤

- Encinitas Board Riders Club is formed to compete in the WCBR contest and also "to support, build and protect our local coastal environment and surf history".
- Moonlight Beach Marine Safety Center at Moonlight Beach is dedicated in May. This $3.9 million-dollar project replaces the old 1952 wooden structure. In addition, a collaborative project with ocean artist Peggy Sue Zepeda with Bob Zepeda doing the finish work for this 8'x15' mosaic titled "Pacific Playground".

2018-19 ➤

- Cardiff State Beach Living Shoreline Project Dedication was held on May 22nd, 2019. This coastal protection project with extensive dune planting will help retain and protect the beach from tidal erosion and loss of sand, especially during the winter tides.

2019 ➤

- Harbaugh Seaside Trails begins construction on March 1st. The area had been purchased by the San Elijo Lagoon Conservancy in 2012. It is an extensive project of a three-acre overlook gateway of Solana Beach extending north to the Cardiff-by-the-Sea trail formerly known as Carpentier Parkway. It is planned to be completed in early 2020 and will showcase a donor monument, viewing deck and a railroad under-crossing into the San Elijo Ecological Reserve. As a land trust, "years of fund raising and strengthening of community has come to fruition."
- Coastal Rail Trail opens to the public on May 9th. The 1.3-mile trail runs from Chesterfield Avenue to the pedestrian crossing at Santa Fe Drive into downtown Encinitas. Described as a "pedestrian and cycle friendly thoroughfare." This is just a portion of the planned forty-four-mile bike-way, which will eventually run from Oceanside to the downtown San Diego Santa Fe Depot.
- Chesterfield Avenue Crossing at San Elijo in Cardiff-by-the-Sea is complete as well as the much-needed rail line double tracking. It is now the first "quiet zone."
- Dickinson Family Education Conservatory (230 Quail Gardens Drive) is completed. Located within the Hamilton Children's Garden, this 8,232-square-foot glass educational facility also offers seating for 265 in the amphitheater.
- San Elijo Lagoon Double Tracking Project gets underway. A new railroad bridge is complete in Cardiff-by-the-Sea. This 72.8 million dollar project is expected to be completed in approximately two years and will stretch 1.5 miles.

*Swami's Beach.*

COURTESY OF KYLE THOMAS PHOTOGRAPHY

✧

*Top: 2019 Saw an E-Bike (Electric Bike) Explosion.*

IMAGE COURTESY OF DAPHNE FLETCHER.

*Below: Biergarten Downtown Encinitas*

IMAGE COURTESY OF NEAL GLASGOW.

- Boathouses (726 & 732 3rd Street) on October 12th are dedicated with an historical bronze plaque provided by the local chapter of the E Clampus Vitus organization. Working with Encinitas Preservation Association (EPA) and Encinitas Historical Society (EHS) and with aid from the City of Encinitas, these iconic boats will now be listed on the National Register of Historic Places.
- "Boutique Luxury Hotel" begins construction on the 4.3-acre property on the northern bluff in Leucadia. Forty-five thousand cubic yards of sand was relocated to the beach below. The planned 226,000-square-foot building complex will boast 130 rooms (including 16 suites) and currently has an estimated cost of $110 million. Owners envision guests walking around in swimsuits, shorts and flip-flops, keeping with the Leucadia beach "vibe." Marketing materials describe the hotel as "barefoot luxury."
- Population is 63,184.

2020 ➤

- Cylovia comes for the first time to downtown Coast Highway 101 on Sunday, January 12 as a no-cars approach to downtown shopping.
- Dunham House built in 1885 on 10th Street, Del Mar, moves to the San Dieguito Heritage Museum in December. The house is named after Edward and Lovey Dunham who lived in the house from 1925 to 1975. The structure is literally sawed in half to 14ft. X 28ft sections and the roof was removed to accommodate the eight-mile trip.

## What is Cyclovia Encinitas?

Cyclovia is a Spanish term that means "Cycleway". This type of event includes the closing of certain streets to automobiles for a temporary time, in order to allow cyclists, skaters, and pedestrians access to local businesses on open streets. In January 2020 Encinitas hosted its first Cyclovia event, and was deemed a total success, with hundreds of participating residents this "all wheels" event. In 2021 the event went "virtual" to keep the momentum going due to the COVID pandemic. Just like the inaugural live event held in 2020, it remains the City's goal to put on an energetic, educational community celebration promoting healthy, active lifestyles, and self-powered transportation in a fun, but virtual way rolling all the way through 2021.

Virtual Cyclovia Encinitas kicked off on Sunday, January 17, 2021 with the launch of the first wave of social media content and an official city-sponsored web page, loaded with interactive media, materials and resources.

Following the January kickoff, the City of Encinitas will continue to roll out fun, informative, and engaging content online, here on this page, and via social media (Facebook, Instagram, Nextdoor, Twitter) with the goal of also offering limited live/in-person features as much as possible throughout 2021 as County Health Orders allow.

*Above and below: Surfing Madonna Beach Run and Half Marathon in 2017 earned the new Guinness Book of World Records title after more than 4,000 people ran across the sands of Moonlight Beach." The Carlsbad Encina Power Plant's smokestack in the background was demolished after a 50-year history in the spring of 2021.*

*Above: Coaster train heading north from San Diego across the San Elijo Lagoon.*

PHOTO COURTESY OF KYLE THOMAS PHOTOGRAPHY

*Left: Helena Holleran and the Nu Funk Shui.*

PHOTO COURTESY OF COLIN LEIBOLD.

*Encinitas Holiday Parade 2019.*

PHOTOGRAPHS BY DAPHNE FLETCHER.

✧

*Encinitas Holiday Parade 2019. No one yet knew it would be the last big event for a very long time.*

PHOTOGRAPHS BY DAPHNE FLETCHER.

*Article reprint courtesy of Encinitas Magazine Editor in Chief Chris Cote.*

IMAGES COURTESY OF KYLE THOMAS.

## THE ROCK 'N' ROLL HOUSE

The Rock 'n' Roll House was once located between A and B Streets, in the alley, west of the Coast Highway, near Moonlight Beach on the property where The Lofts at Moonlight Beach now stand. It was a small two-story apartment whose entire structure, along with the garage, yard and even the telephone pole, was transformed into a crazy, wildly psychedelic piece of art by the apartment's resident, Richard Margolin.

"It began mysteriously and unpredictable," says Richard. "I had never done art in my life. I was 56 years old, living in a motel room in Oceanside, and if somebody would have said, "You're an artist", I would have told them, "What the hell are you talking about!"

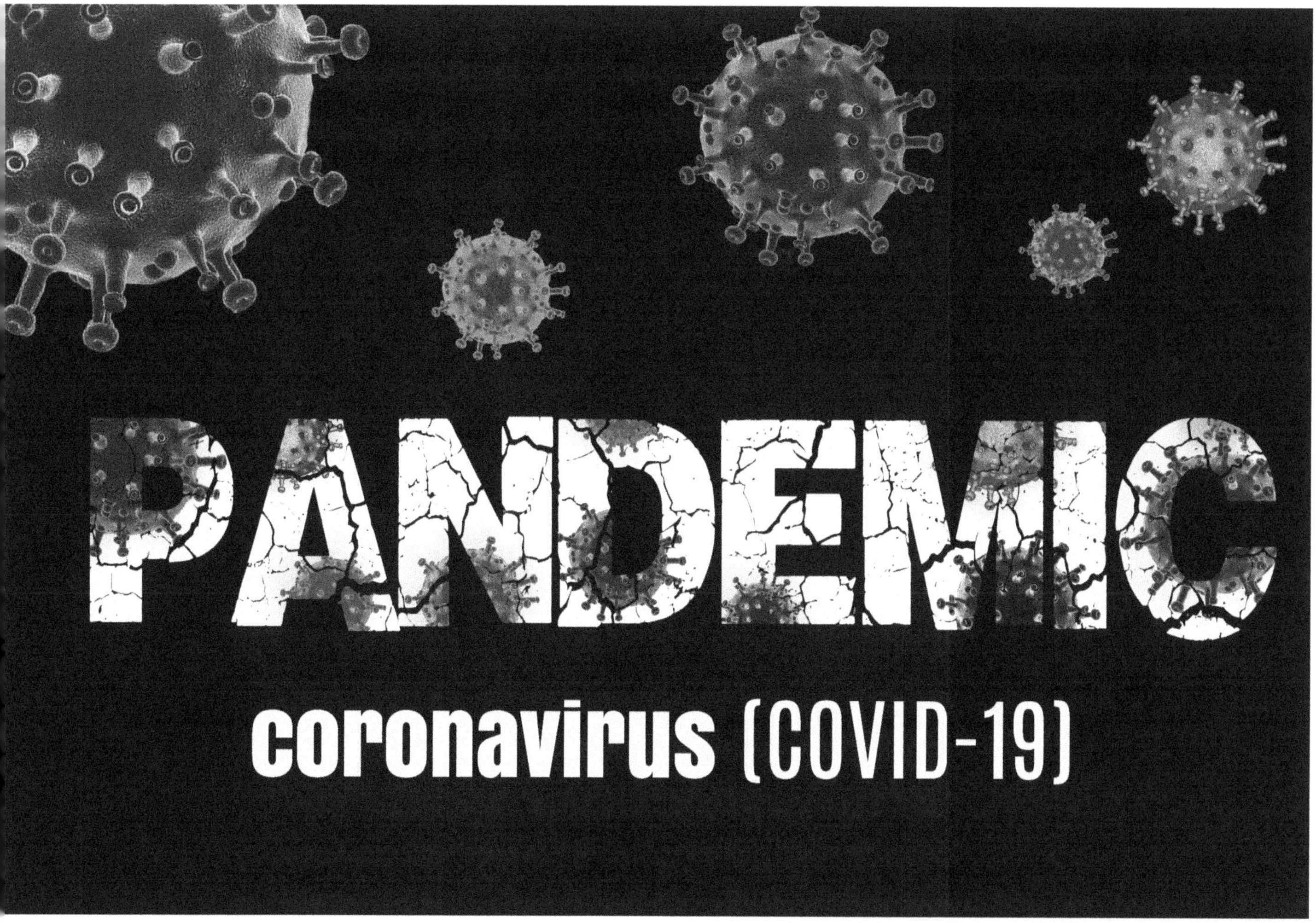

# Chapter 9

## Encinitas and the Coronavirus

IMAGE COURTESY OF DEPOSIT PHOTOS ID #360151110.

2020 Coronavirus, COVID-19 Pandemic statistics start being recorded on January 20th in the United States. It is believed the origin of this new virus is Wuhan, China, first reported in December 2019. This purportedly resulted from humans ingesting exotic wildlife from an open market located there. Some other reports reveal the virus might have been created in a laboratory. It is declared a worldwide pandemic.

By March the United States issues quarantine rules to stop its spread and closes its borders. California's governor, Gavin Newsom, is the first in the nation to completely "lock-down" the state by closing borders, businesses, schools, beaches, parks and theaters causing panic buying at the grocery stores clearing shelves and causing shortages and rationing. All concerts, sporting and cultural events are immediately canceled. Air travel is limited, and cruise lines are shut down. Nursing homes are in also in total lock-down, with meals being served in residents' private apartments. School and church services at first are held outside, later not at all—only by "Zoom" which becomes the new meeting norm—an online digital meeting app which prior to the pandemic was barely heard of. Grocery stores offer on-line orders and/or delivery.

In late spring, beaches and parks open back up. Coronavirus outbreaks continue despite the lock-down and new rules are set in place by individual state governors. California's governor mandates protective facial masks to be worn for any activity outside the home. All public gatherings continue

to be canceled: weddings, graduations, funerals and family reunions have either been canceled, postponed or have severely limited attendance. Pharmaceutical companies fast-track testing kits to offer the public.

Covid-19 testing becomes required prior to any medical procedure and international flights, with many countries restricting admission from the United States due to the highest case levels in the world by the end of 2020. Schools conduct classes online, and sports events hold games but with no audience. All meetings are now conducted via webinars and/or Zoom set up on computers, iPads, or smart phones. School hours are extremely limited on campus, as most lessons are conducted online.

Late in 2020, several pharmaceutical companies tout the effectiveness of their vaccine and push for approval for mass inoculations as the cases are increasing and the death toll rises. Thanksgiving is mandated as having no more than three households in attendance by the state of California. Restaurant restrictions are eased to allow outdoor dining only. The Encinitas Fall Street Fair and Holiday Parade are canceled. By December 14, the first inoculation was administered to a health care provider in New York.

To be continued...."

*Airports became ghost towns as air travel, both domestic and international, was severely curtailed.*

PHOTOS COURTESY OF DAPHNE FLETCHER.

*Mask wearing and disruptions to daily life became the "new" norm. Hoarding toilet paper subsided as people adjusted to the new norm.*

PHOTOS COURTESY OF DEPOSIT PHOTOS ID #6511819, 359940774 AND 357921970.

*Tempers flared as aspects of the pandemic overturned daily life. Zoom became a popular way to continue work and connect with family. Children went to school by video classes.*

TOP LEFT AND BOTTOM IMAGE COURTESY OF DAPHNE FLETCHER.

TOP RIGHT IMAGE COURTESY OF DEPOSIT PHOTOS ID #366166490.

CITY OF ENCINITAS
MARINE SAFETY CENTER
BEACHES AND ACCESSES ARE CLOSED
BEACHES AND ACCESSES ARE CLOSED

FACIAL COVERINGS REQUIRED
KEEP 6 FEET APART
NO GATHERING
FACIAL COVERINGS MANDATORY ON STAIRS
SHARE THE ACCESS SAFELY
PROHIBITED BEACH ACTIVITIES
ALLOWED BEACH ACTIVITIES
WEAR FACIAL COVERINGS
REQUIRED
DON'T USE IF YOU'RE SICK
EncinitasCA.Gov for COVID19 updates

CITY OF ENCINITAS
FIRE & MARINE SAFETY DEPARTMENT
BEACHES AND ACCESSES ARE CLOSED
(GOV. CODE SECTION 8665)

✧

*Moonlight Beach D Street looking south toward Swamis Point.*

PHOTO COURTESY OF DAPHNE FLETCHER.

# About the Authors

Carolyn Roy Cope is a second generation local, born in Encinitas in 1950. Her mother, Thelma M. Boggs, was originally from Burlington, Colorado and her father, Gerard E. Roy, immigrated from Quebec, Canada. Both arrived in Encinitas about the same time c.1938.

Carolyn attended all local schools, focusing on journalism, sports and acting. She worked at her family's grocery store, Roy's Market, every day after school. She wrote for her schools' newspapers in middle school, high school, and college. She had a column in the local Coast News for many years called "Cope's Corner". Carolyn has served on the boards of many local organizations in Encinitas: Sister City, Cardiff-by-the-Sea Chamber, San Dieguito Heritage Museum, Arts Commission, Coastal Community Foundation, E-101 Mainstreet, Encinitas Arts Culture and Ecology Alliance and Encinitas Preservation Association. She is currently the President of the Encinitas Historical Society. She is still an active member of the Rotary Club of Encinitas, serving over 20 years. Carolyn is also the well-known voice announcing at the annual Holiday Parade. "I like facts, dates and places. That is why I presented the historical section of this book chronologically."

Born in Whittier, California in 1953, Jim Filanc moved with his family to Encinitas in 1965. A lifelong lover of the outdoors, Jim participated in the Boy Scouts where he earned the rank of Eagle Scout. A 1972 graduate from San Dieguito High School, Jim went on to earn a BS of Finance from San Diego State University in 1976. He has had a varied career working construction. As an avid off-road enthusiast, he raced in the Baja 1000 twice, finishing the second time with his co-captains Malcolm Smith and JN Roberts. He produced a 2008 feature length motion picture called "Full Circle—The Legend Lives On," starring himself along with Smith and Roberts. The movie reunites Smith and Roberts 40 years after their inaugural motorcycle victory in the first Baja 1000 in 1967. He has raised over $100,000 for various charities. Jim is also a musician/songwriter/recording artist, having provided guitar tracks on several released albums. Currently, Jim is President/CEO of his firm, Intelligent Cities Associates, LLC, helping clients plan their "Smart City" future. Finally, for more than 20 years Jim has teamed with Encinitas local, Luis Ortiz, to light up the Encinitas Heritage Tree at Moonlight Beach, emceeing recent tree lighting ceremonies presenting local choirs and singing groups to celebrate the holiday season.

Garth Murphy is a poet, songwriter, journalist and author. His historical novel, The Indian Lover, set in the 1840s of San Diego, explored the cultural clashes of Native American people, the Spanish Colonists Californios and the tidal wave of new American immigrants. The book explores the encompassing height of the Mexican Rancho era, the Mexican-American war of 1846, the international Gold Rush of 1848-49 and the US statehood of California in 1850. Researching with archaeologist James Moriarity made this effort to describe pre-Columbian Encinitas possible.

Mr. Murphy's own role in Encinitas history includes pioneering local surf culture, surf research, developing surfboard wax and the flexible lifeguard rescue buoy. He continues restoration of the 1887 Derby House, built by Miles Kellogg for Amos Derby an early railroad man. He is also instrumental in working with the State of California on the Marine Life Protection Act Initiative. During that time he help design and install a network of marine reserves between Point Conception and the Mexican border. This includes Swamis State Marine Protected Area that runs from Seaside bluff to Moonlight Beach plus San Elijo Lagoon and encompasses three miles off shore. He was also a founding member of The Encinitas Arts Culture and Ecology Alliance and the Pacific View Academy of Arts project in alliance with the City of Encinitas. Mr. Murphy is a long standing member of the Encinitas Historical Society.

# About the Cover

## Kevin Anderson

Kevin Anderson is fascinated with imagery, art, and color. Since his childhood, this fascination has developed into an obsession that went from coloring books and comics, to more refined attempts at art in High School. He studied further into college, and after earning a degree in Fine Art, he began his career as a professional artist. He paints large murals on buildings, as well as commissions on canvas, and outdoor scenes on location. He is always painting and drawing, dreaming of making a significant contribution to the art world, and hopes his artwork keeps developing towards that end.

*Pipes Ramp*

*The cover painting is showing the Cardiff beach known to local surfers as "Pipes Ramp" looking north towards Swami's Point.*

# About the Contributing Photographers

## Daphne Fletcher

Daphne Fletcher, publisher, writer, editor, founder and CEO of Ledge Media, and President of HPN Books, is also an avid travel photographer and has contributed photography to more than a dozen coffee table books she has published. Daphne made a home for herself in Leucadia after falling in love with Encinitas while working on this book. She has become very active in the community serving on the boards of directors for both the Encinitas Rotary Club and the Mainstreet organization Leucadia 101.

## Kyle Thomas Photography

Kyle Thomas is a Multimedia Specialist. He is a fourth-generation San Diegan, and a professional journalist and photographer who loves to bring history to the San Diego County public through writing, photography, and videography. He has been a regular contributor of stories and pictures to Encinitas Magazine since it's inception. Kyle grew up in Clairemont, moved to Del Mar at age fifteen, and then to Encinitas shortly thereafter, where he attended San Dieguito High School graduating with the class of 1975.

## Neal Glasgow Photography

Neal Glasgow is a Cardiff/Encinitas native who is continuing his exploration in art through photography. He graduated from San Dieguito High School. Over his career as both an artist and an art educator, he has focused on a variety of creative pathways, subject matter, and techniques. He returned to his alma mater to teach art and science for sixteen years.

www.ingramcontent.com/pod-product-compliance
Lightning Source LLC
Chambersburg PA
CBHW041833110726
48006CB00020B/2609
*9798891770034*